THOMAS CHAMBERS HINE

An Architect of Victorian Nottingham

Ken Brand

1. INTRODUCTION - His Early Life

It is sometimes said that the first effects of newly acquired wealth are always seen in the buildings of a town. This is undoubtedly true of Nottingham, which underwent a vast expansion in the 19th century. The population rose from 28,801 (1801) to 213,877 (1891), and its size increased from 1,996 to 10,935 acres. By 1850 industry, particularly the lace industry, was flourishing. Business was good; the world wanted Nottingham lace and Nottingham obliged. New factories, warehouses and later splendid dwellings for the successful industrialists provided local architects with tremendous opportunities to reveal their skill, flair and imagination. Not surprisingly some were more successful than others, but none was more successful in Nottingham from the middle part of the century than Thomas Chambers Hine. When he died in 1899 his colleagues properly and affectionately knew him as "the father of the Midland Architects".

Thomas Chambers Hine was born in Southampton Street, Covent Garden, London on May 31 1813, the eldest son of Jonathan Hine, a Nottingham hosiery manufacturer, and Mary Chambers, the daughter of a hosiery merchant. His parents were married on 27th December 1803. The family must have spent periods in London for throughout his life Hine was always proud to recall that he was taken, in his nurse's arms, onto the ice of the Thames when it was frozen over in 1814. His maternal grandfather was Thomas Chambers (d. 1811) who started work as a framework knitter and progressed to be a hosiery merchant, being the senior partner of Chambers, Wilson and Morley. From this business came the noted I. & R. Morley Company.

The Hines were a prosperous commercial middle-class family. Jonathan Hine (1780-1862), who arrived in Nottingham in February 1795, came from an old Dorset family centred on Beaminster. One family member, another Thomas, left Beaminster for France in 1792 at the age of 17 years. He obtained employment in a winery in Jarnac and in time married the boss's daughter thus giving the family name to a cognac producer in Jarnac. There is at least one Hine still involved in running the firm. The Beaminster museum has a section devoted to the Hine family.

Thomas Chambers Hine received little formal education, but displayed some aptitude for draughtsmanship and an interest in architecture and history. This fondness for local history was to last throughout his life. His own skill as an illustrator was first acknowledged in 1840 when his fanciful reconstruction of Nottingham Castle in the 16th century was used as a frontispiece for the second volume of James Orange's 'History of Nottingham'; it was often reproduced and adapted later.

Traditionally the eldest son always went into the family firm, but Hine's flair for drawing and architecture led to his being articled to the London architect Matthew Habershon (1789-1852). In his office Hine got a thorough grounding in all types of building practice: Gothic churches, Italianate warehouses and villas, schools and hospitals. A fellow pupil who became a life-long friend was the London architect Ewan Christian (1814-95) who specialised in restoring village churches. Habershon was the architect of Derby Town Hall (1828, now Guildhall and partly rebuilt), so Hine is likely to have become familiar with the designs, although he was only 15 years old at the time.

2. In Partnership and Practice

In 1834 Hine finished his training in London and returned to Nottingham. For a period around 1835 Thomas Hine is listed as both architect and builder with an address: Nottingham Terrace, Park, (later Park Terrace). He formally entered into a partnership with William Patterson, a builder, of St. James's Street and Park on 4th August 1834. In Orange's Directory of 1840, Patterson and Hine are classified as both "Architects and Surveyors" and as "Builders", of St. James's Street.

On 16th February 1837 Hine married Mary Betts of Stamford; his eldest grandson recalled this as an elopement. Their wedding trip - honeymoon - took in Leicester, Leamington, Birmingham and Ashby and they returned on 24 February. The census return for 1841 has the Hine family living at an unnumbered address in St. James's Street. The household comprised Thomas, aged 28 (erroneously given as 25), his wife Mary (28) and two daughters Mary (2) and Sarah (1). There were two young female servants.

Patterson was the builder of the Regency semi-detached houses, now 1-12 Park Terrace, completed c.1833. No doubt young Hine, living in or near these houses, was impressed by the way they straddled the sandstone rim of the Park. His admiration for the combined skills of the architect and his builder was later reflected in the way he tackled projects on unprepossessing sites. The architect here was almost certainly Peter Frederick Robinson (1776-1858), architect to the 4th Duke of Newcastle between 1825 and the late 1830s. Hine might have checked out his earlier work in Leamington whilst on his wedding trip. Thomas Winter, an architect and surveyor of Rutland Street, Standard Hill, employed in that capacity and as local agent by the Duke, no doubt assisted Robinson.

Little is known of Hine's years with Patterson; their first buildings appear to be the school and parsonage at Stapleford, Nottinghamshire in 1836. In later years Hine recalled some of his early work, on the 7th December 1837 he made a design for Whatton Hall (Manor), which with Broughton Hall "were my first mansions." In 1838 they erected the stuccoed Georgian style rectory at Averham, Nottinghamshire. On 19th June 1844 he completed designs for Shirebrook Church, Derbyshire. ("My first church"), built by C. Lindley, it was consecrated on 9th October 1844. At the end of that year he prepared designs for the former Grammar School, Sheffield Road, Chesterfield. It was his first school, built by a Mr Rollinson, and completed in 1846. In August of that year he drew up plans for his first factory, Pleasley Mill. He formally signed the dissolution of the partnership with William Patterson on 31st March 1849.

However, during this time in the partnership Hine would have been in a position to get his name known. In addition he had the opportunity of observing several nationally known architects at work locally, notably Augustus Welby Pugin on St. Barnabas, Derby Road (1841-44), George Gilbert Scott and W.B. Moffatt on St. John's, Leenside (1843) and St. Mary's, (1843-48) and Peter Frederick Robinson on Park Valley (c. 1838-39).

There is a suspicion that Hine embarked upon his own projects several years before parting company with Patterson. Most relevantly he started designing his own house, which included his drawing office, for a site at the junction of Regent Street and Oxford Street then known as Reservoir Street and South Circus Street respectively. The plot of land with an area of 486 square yards was initially sold at auction in July 1844. It is a very narrow and steeply sloping site and must have been considered very difficult to develop, as it was soon back on the market. Hine, liking a challenge, saw potential in the site and on 19th September 1845 paid a deposit on the land, which he later purchased from Messrs Parsons for £218. Work on the house proceeded rapidly and it was completed by October 1846 at a cost of £1,053. Thus in Lascelles and Hagar's Directory of 1848 his entry is "Hine Thomas Chambers *architect*, h South Circus street", having been listed as living in St. James's Street in White's 1844 Directory. Meanwhile his partner Patterson had moved to Burton Joyce.

Hine's house,
25 REGENT STREET,
the family home from
its completion in 1846
until the architect's
death in 1899.
His drawing office is
to the right

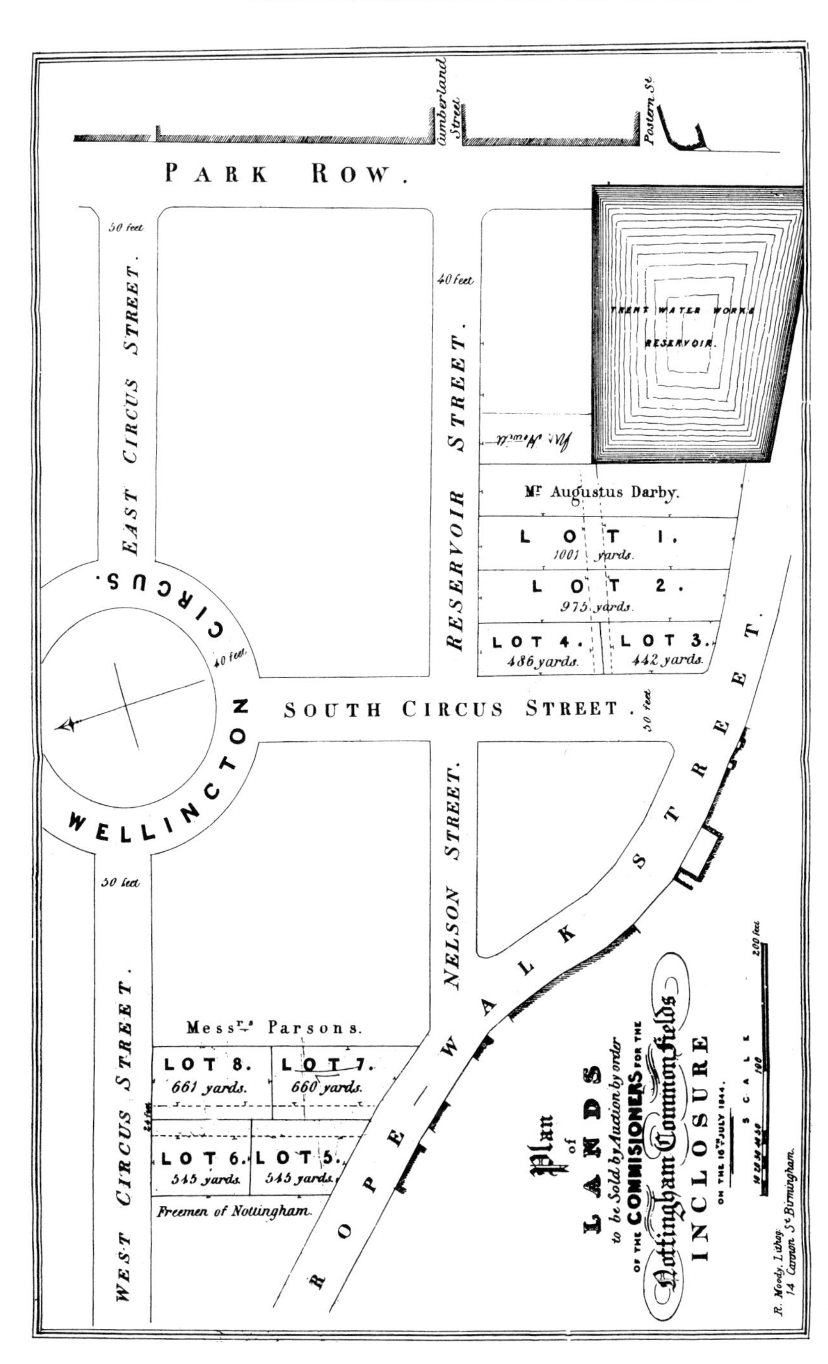

A Plan of Lands sold at auction by the Commissioners for the Nottingham Common Fields Inclosure at the George IV Hotel on 16 July 1844. The plot that Hine later purchased from Messrs Parsons in September 1845 for £218, is that marked LOT 4, at the junction of Reservoir Street and South Circus Street. (N.R.O.)

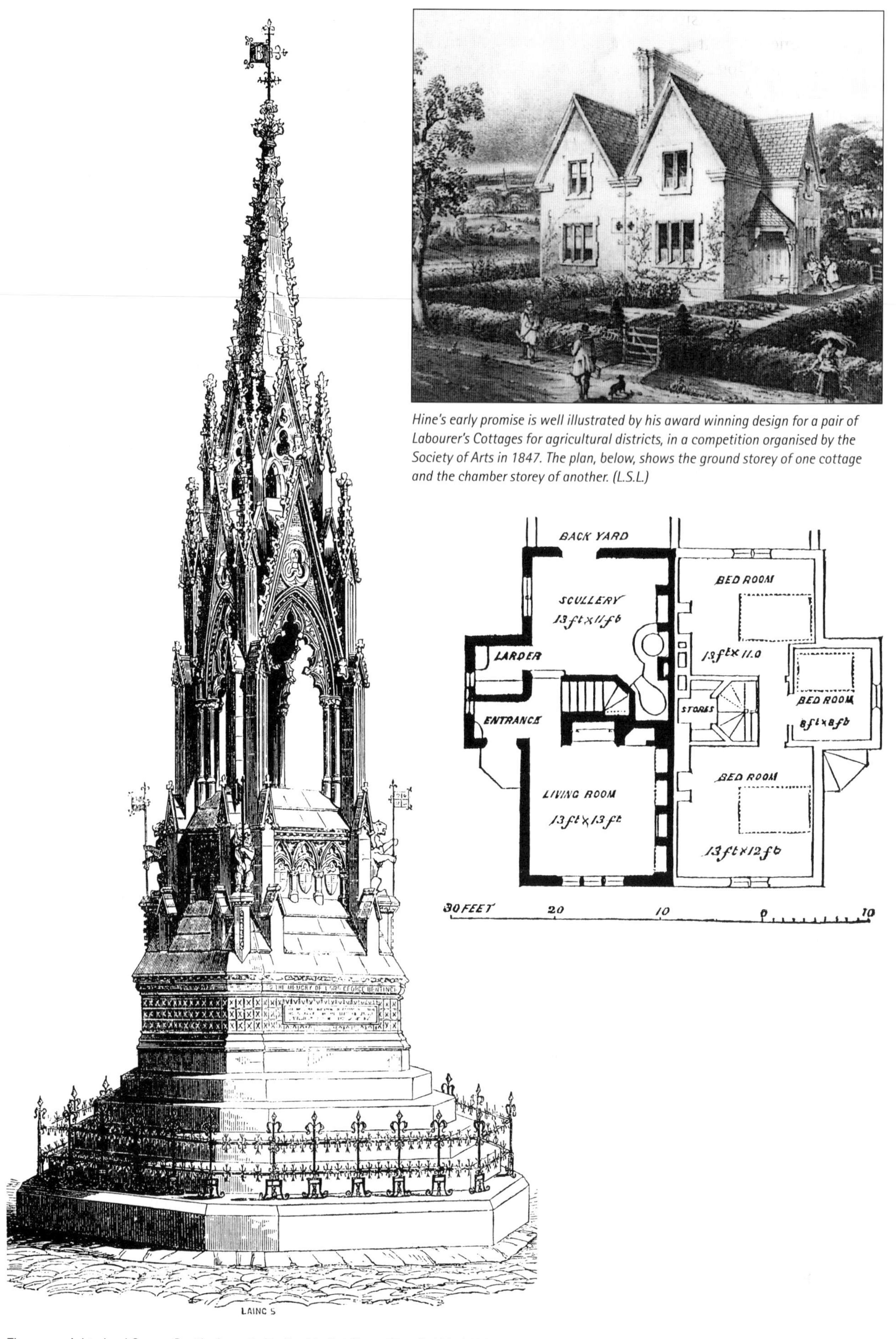

Hine's early promise is well illustrated by his award winning design for a pair of Labourer's Cottages for agricultural districts, in a competition organised by the Society of Arts in 1847. The plan, below, shows the ground storey of one cottage and the chamber storey of another. (L.S.L.)

The memorial to Lord George Bentinck erected in the Market Place, Mansfield in 1849. Hine's design was based on the Queen Eleanor crosses. (L.S.L.)

In the 1851 census return Hine is listed as an architect with four clerks. The street has been renamed Regent Street, though the house is not numbered. Besides his wife Mary, his family consists of four daughters and a son: Mary now aged 12, Sarah 11, George Thomas 9, Emily 7, and Annie 2. A governess, nursemaid, cook, and housemaid catered for their needs. His practice is located at the house.

The house, now No. 25 Regent Street, was of somewhat unusual design, featuring a tower with a pattern of blue bricks here picking out the initials T.H. This feature, known as diapering and copied from Tudor buildings, reappears in many later designs and helps to identify his work. Other features, including kneeler stones and lugged stone framed windows; facets of his later domestic style, appear here. The interior of No. 25 was Gothic, yet contained one of the first water closets in Nottingham. Hine's eldest grandson, C. Carew-Webb, writing in 1949 when he was 83, recalled it "as a most beautiful house and comfortable in every way". He says that his grandfather "always prided himself on being up-to-date, especially in matters of sanitation", although as the pipes went through the middle of the house he added "All my life I can remember a musty smell, especially in the pantry".

The success with his own house must have reassured Hine later when faced with the challenge of difficult sites. The Park has several examples of his unique skill in utilizing the most unlikely plots. As his grandson put it, Hine seemed "to get pleasure and satisfaction and perhaps amusement in putting up houses on difficult and unpromising sites".

The Victorian architect reached his clients by a network of personal contacts and recommendations, through publishing a book or by being featured in the architectural press, often *The Builder*, founded in 1842 and soon afterwards *Building News* and *The Architect*. All of these openings helped Hine early in his own practice, as did occasionally the popular *Illustrated London News*.

He first got his name in the national press in 1848 by winning an open competition for a pair of Labourers' Cottages for agricultural districts costing not more than £300. This competition, organised by the Society of Arts in 1847, attracted 61 entries. The *Illustrated London News* in its issue of June 17th, 1848, (p.393) gave the winning entry such favourable publicity that Hine received many postal requests for details of these cottages. He responded quickly by publishing a short monograph entitled "Prize Model Cottage: Detailed Working Drawings, Plans, Sections and Elevations of a Design for Labourers' Cottages . . . Accompanied by a Specification". Hine's design was technically very advanced, including underfloor heating, yet the outside appearance was of an orthodox three bedroomed country estate cottage in the Tudor style. Even so the estimated cost for the pair, at about £285 in the Midland counties, was within the specified limit. Later in the year he produced an enlarged edition, which included the design of the second prize-winner, I.C. Nichol of London. Hine went to London on 29 June to receive his prize, which was given by Prince Albert.

This was an incredibly fortunate boost for a rising architect, aged 35, just starting his own office. Visible patronage of the nobility soon followed. The 4th Duke of Portland, through the Duke of Newcastle, invited him to design a memorial to his son Lord George Bentinck who had died suddenly whilst walking through the park at Welbeck at the end of September 1848. He first visited the Duke at Clumber to discuss the memorial on 7th April 1849, followed by further visits on 23rd April and 25th August. Originally various propositions were considered among which were a new wing to the General Hospital at Nottingham, and a monument in Southwell Minster. Hine's design was based on the Queen Eleanor crosses in the Decorated style of architecture. The 52 feet high monument is divided into three stages: a base or pedestal; a gabled canopy; and a spire topped by a weather vane. It was erected in the Market Place, Mansfield late in 1849. The contractor was Mr. C. Lindley of Mansfield.

It is likely that Hine had already started his long working association with the Newcastle family. He is considered to have been the architect of houses on Park Valley and Western Terrace in the 4th Duke's Park Estate completed in the late 1840s. Other early works for the Duke included Maplebeck Parsonage (1849) near Southwell.

His reputation, built up during his association with Patterson, brought early work to his new practice; as architect, the design of Kinoulton Rectory (1849); and as surveyor the inspection of the chancel roof of Newark Church (1848).

An important early commission for Hine was the Nottingham Corn Exchange (1849-50) in Thurland Street, on part of the site of the old Thurland Hall, Newcastle property, which had been demolished in 1831. It appears to be his first major commercial building in Nottingham. It was on this building that Hine developed his combination of Italian Renaissance and English Jacobean, to produce what he called Anglo-Italian. Here were included for the first time the distinctive mullioned and transomed windows, which became a favourite characteristic of his commercial style. The decoration of the building included a frieze of encaustic tiles at first floor level and patterned brickwork above and below the cornice. Contemporary accounts suggest that part of Hine's inspiration for the Corn Exchange came from Sir William Wilson's design for the Grammar School at Appleby Parva, Leicestershire, (1693-7). For £3,000 the architect provided a principal room 77ft by 40ft by 40ft high and a number of offices. It was opened on 6th April 1850.

In 1846 Albert Street was constructed to link Wheeler Gate with Lister Gate, and another of Hine's early works was to build the houses and shops on its west side, abutting on the cemetery of Castle Gate chapel. These have since been refronted or demolished for road widening and his work is no longer discernible here, though a warehouse for the hosiery manufacturer William Gibson built by Hine about 1854 can be seen opposite at the junction of Low Pavement and Lister Gate. It closely resembles his Lace Market work of the time but is now rather poorly refaced.

The family hosiery firm of Hine and Mundella Ltd. commissioned Hine's first factory in the town. Its opening was marked by a soirée held on 3rd October 1851 and organized by the staff as a tribute to the directors. Speeches and toasts were a feature of the evening. In a short speech prior to proposing a toast to the architect, the non-family director Anthony John Mundella made perceptive comments about the building and its architect. "This building makes no pretension to beauty. Nothing has been expended on ornament, but I believe it is its own ornament. To my mind, its fitness and adaptability to the purposes required and its strength and security are its ornament. Appreciating as I do his laborious and intense exertions which have been bestowed, not only on the grander features of the scheme, but upon the details, the minor matters not usually included in the architect's duties even to the fixing of machinery, I shall esteem him as long as memory retains her seat."

The building Hine produced was a five-storeyed building in the Westcroft (Station Street), notable for being the first factory to have steam-operated stocking frames. Externally the factory was like the letter 'L', 192 feet by 120 feet. The longer frontage contained the warehouse, the shorter the factory. The rooms were wide and spacious and lit from floor to ceiling. A topical design point of the day was the use of "iron columns similar to those, which grace the Crystal Palace."

In Eliza Cook's Journal (May 15th, 1852) this new species of factory was described thus ". . there was not only cleanliness and light but elegance, about that which I had been led to consider all smoke and uncleanliness". This building was largely destroyed by fire on February 1st, 1859. It seems likely that T.C. Hine was responsible for rebuilding the factory, which in 1864 became part of Nottingham Manufacturing; in later years the building became part of the Station Street factory complex of Boots. It was finally demolished in the 1970s.

3. A Versatile Architect

A decade of intense activity involving very varied challenges followed. In the early 1850s Hine began to get commissions for modernising country houses, starting with the complicated rebuilding of Ogston Hall in Derbyshire between 1851-64 with the inevitable tower, which still remains although the conservatory of 1860 is now in ruins. As Pevsner implied, Hine Victorianised it for Gladwin Turbutt. In 1852 he built a tower on to a small hunting lodge for John Francklin Esq. at Gonalston Hall near Southwell, and enlarged the early 18th century South Manor at Ruddington for Sir Thomas Parkyns.

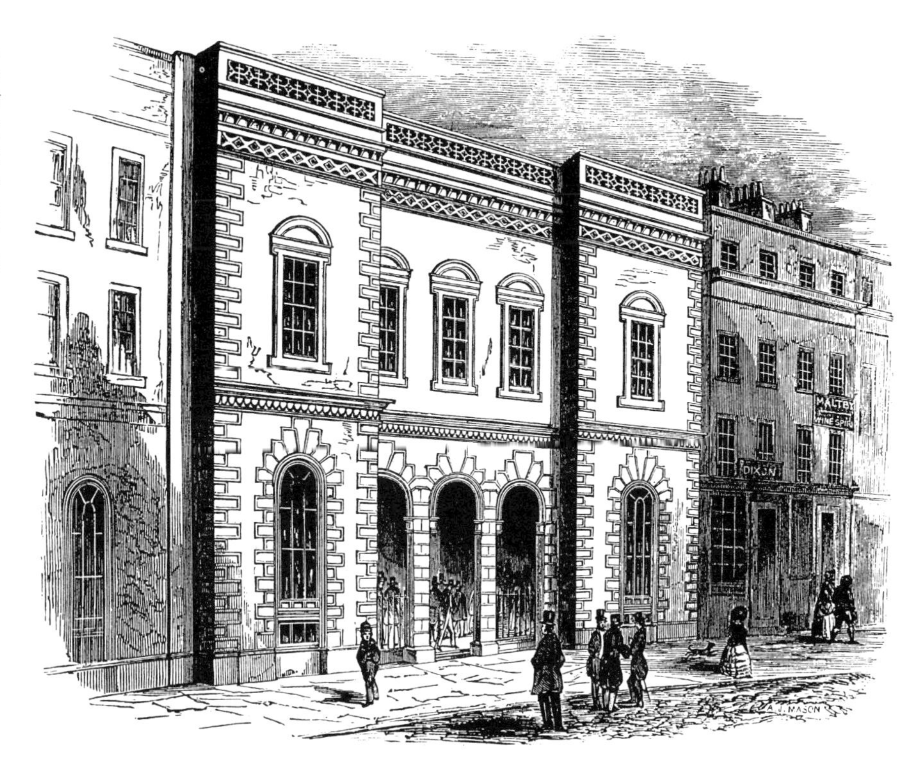

The Nottingham Corn Exchange, Thurland Street, which opened in 1850 displays Hine's early use of quoins, encaustic tiles and patterned brickwork. In recent years it has undergone many changes, the latest being bar/restaurants "stone" and "Obsession". (L.S.L.)

The Station Street entrance to the premises of B.H. Hine and Mundella & Co. (1851) "It was one of the first of those palatial erections we may almost say, by Mr. T.C. Hine...which have made Nottingham factories and warehouses celebrated for their scale and beauty throughout the country." It burnt down in 1859 and later rebuilt. (L.S.L.)

Part of Hine's splendid terrace 2-12 Regent Street, erected in the mid 1850s. Alternate pairs are set back, which allows the introduction of quoins, whilst all have Georgian windows, shaped gables and simulated strap work.

Perhaps the most important commission at this time was the work carried out at Flintham Hall, Nottinghamshire between 1851-57 for T.B.T. Hildyard Esq., MP. The old house was partly encased in a variation of the Anglo-Italian style, a tower was added and the interior alterations produced a fine two-storey library leading to a unique tall brick palm house with a semi-circular glass roof. This conservatory, complete with statuary and fountain, was surely inspired by Paxton's Crystal Palace and his glasshouses at Chatsworth. Queen Victoria opened the Great Exhibition on 1st May 1851. Before the end of the month, on 30th May, Hine started a five-day visit to the exhibition.

The north lodge at Flintham Hall, whilst detached, incorporates several features from Hine's award-winning design for labourers' cottages. The west lodge with its shaped gables also by Hine probably owes much to the architect's acquaintance with John Loudon's encyclopaedia of 1833.

Hine developed both sides of Regent Street during the 1850s. These buildings survive and well illustrate his early domestic styles. On the south side No. 7-15, completed by 1854, form a tall Jacobean terrace with shaped gables. The northern side between Park Row and Oxford Street, completed by 1858, is essentially two distinct terraces linked by No. 14 with its two tier bay windows. Nos. 2-12 have flamboyant Elizabethan facades with shaped gables, simulated strap-work and quoins. To enliven a flat elevation Hine cleverly set back No. 6-8, allowing the introduction of extra quoins to telling effect. No. 16-24 present a more rectangular appearance, yet ample use of stone dressings, door frames borrowed from his commercial style and dormer windows set in Anglo-Italianate gables, give this terrace a certain exuberance. No. 28 and No. 28a, turning into Oxford Street, dated 1858 (and in 1875 the first home of the High School for Girls) continue the use of quoins but the parapet is reminiscent of the Corn Exchange. No. 27 Regent Street (c. 1860) further up and nearer the junction with The Ropewalk, was built in the Swiss style and embellished with a rich variety of decorative stonework. Hine was also the architect of houses in Oxford Street (No. 10, c.1859), East Circus Street, Wellington Circus, College Street (No. 1 dated 1851), Upper College Street and The Ropewalk in the 1850s. No. 30-36 Regent Street could probably be added to this list.

An unsubstantiated reference indicated that sometime early in 1852 Hine tackled the opposite end of the housing market. An undated report from the *Nottingham Review* indicated ". . . the only approach to cheap houses on the newly enclosed lands are some now erecting in the Meadows, from plans prepared by Mr. T.C. Hine, which adopt the back-to-back system, but obviate all its objections".

In 1853 the Bluecoat School moved out of its cramped premises on High Pavement, facing Garners Hill, to new buildings on Mansfield Road (now the International Community Centre). Hine was chosen as architect and designed the new school in the Elizabethan style with gables and mullioned windows. The two statues of the traditionally dressed Bluecoat pupils were copied by a local sculptor, J. Stonehouse, from those of the old building and placed in specially prepared corner niches. Facing the school across Mansfield Road were two houses, each with distinctive Hine gables and blue brick patterning which could be of about the same date. They survived until the site was redeveloped in the late 1980s.

A much smaller school was built at Epperstone in 1854 where Hine also provided a house for the Huskinson family.

A different project was the building of the St. George's Hall at a cost of £7,000 at the western end of Parliament Street, a site occupied by the former Co-op department store. This was a music hall in the Elizabethan style with an impressive semi-circular end facing Derby Road and windows from his Lace Market vein. Here again Hine employed Stonehouse to provide decorative statuary. It opened in May 1854 with a charity concert in aid of families of soldiers serving in the Crimean War. The hall was demolished in 1902 when Parliament Street was widened to allow the passage of electric trams from Derby Road round onto Parliament Street. Hine appears to have been greatly moved by the Crimean War. On 13 May 1856 he proposed, unsuccessfully, the erection of a local memorial to the War. In its issue of 16 May 1856 the *Nottingham Review* carried a description of the civic procession around the town celebrating the end of the war. It noted "But by far the most beautiful sight in the whole route was the general aspect in Regent Street...At the corner of the offices of Mr. T.C. Hine was a display equally light and beautiful, and was suitable and effective; the drapery represented purple and gold, so hung as to form the most graceful folds, garnished with flowers, evergreens, and ribbons-the word "Peace" formed by evergreens, surmounting the whole."

The opening of the Bluecoat School, Mansfield Road, (now the International Community Centre) in July 1853, as shown in a contemporary illustration. (L.S.L.)

St. George's Hall, Parliament Street and Derby Road. Hine's warehouse style can be seen in this Music Hall erected in 1853-4 at a cost of £7,000. It was demolished in 1902 in order to allow the passage of electric trams from Derby Road round onto Parliament Street. (L.S.L.)

4. The Lace Market, Nottingham

Some of the most important examples of Hine's work can be seen in the Lace Market, in its way a triumph of small-scale townscape. The 1850s was Hine's great decade and during the years 1853-6 he redefined and elevated the status of the area. In the early 1840s there were two groups of warehouses in the town, the older centred on Hounds Gate and the newer on St. Mary's Gate. By 1847 the local press had concluded that "Mary Gate" was the seat of the Lace Market. Here the premises were either quite modest with "Plain brick frontages, with small square headed windows and low ill-ventilated rooms", or they were converted abandoned mansions of the gentry. In the latter case the owner often lived upstairs. Here were to be found two of the later great names in the lace trade. Thomas Adams, then of Adams, Page and Cullen, St Mary's Gate and St. Mary's Place, and Richard Birkin of Mallet and Birkin, St Mary's Gate.

Then Hine arrived with his new generation of warehouses creating exciting new buildings for both Birkin and Adams. Hine was modestly aware of the impact his work was making. As he observed at the opening of the enormous new Adams and Page warehouse on 10 July 1855: "Of the twelve new warehouses, which I have erected in this town since 1851 I may venture to say that this is the largest, and, as an architectural work, perhaps the most important, and will with the other new warehouses and factories erected during the same time, hereafter mark a most important period in the commercial history of the town."

The old Plumptre House, fronting onto Stoney Street and adjoining the northern side of St. Mary's churchyard, was designed by Colen Campbell from 1724, but completed c.1730 under the guidance of Mr Plumptre, after Campbell's death in 1729. The Plumptres had long abandoned it when Richard Birkin purchased the house and grounds at auction in February 1853 for £8,410. Hine was engaged and that autumn started to cut a new street, Broadway, through the grounds. His subtle trick of placing a double curve in its centre created the illusion, with his tall warehouses; of a canyon-like cul-de-sac when viewed from either the St. Mary's Gate or Stoney Street end.

Broadway was essentially, but not entirely, associated with the Birkin family, Richard and his sons Richard and Thomas Isaac. Richard Birkin first entered the lace trade in Basford at the time of the twist net fever 1823-5 and survived the inevitable slump. By innovation and business acumen he prospered, particularly in association with Alderman Biddle. Such was his standing in the lace trade that he was a judge at the 1851 Exhibition. He maintained his manufacturing base in Basford, while his new warehouses on Broadway provided easy access for buyers and marketing generally. Richard promoted his sons as partners in 1852 whilst he retired just as the new warehouses were completed. Besides being a long serving Alderman, he was four times Mayor of Nottingham

Above the gateway of the Birkin suite of four warehouses on the southern side of Broadway is the Bee emblem above Birkin's initials and the date **18:R:B:55**. Flanking this to the left dipping down in a stone ribbon are the son's initials RB (R being reversed) and then T.C.H. and an architect's motif of dividers and square. Similarly to the right are first the other son's initials TB followed by the builder's initials G. and H. (Garland and Holland) and a builder's motif of hammer and trowel. Within the archway, on the right, built into the wall, is an earlier stone plaque carrying the coat of arms of the Plumptre family and below, two small 12th century arches, probably from the earlier 12th century St. Mary's Church and stored after rebuilding. The building of the warehouses was not without difficulty owing to the discovery of an ancient tiered cave system under some of the new buildings. The completion of the Birkin warehouses appears to slightly predate that of the Adams and Page warehouse, although Plumptre House survived a little longer, for the Government School of Design had a temporary home there until at least November 1855. In recent years Broadway has had numerous tenants, but now with some buildings converted into apartments and others into bars and clubs and New College Nottingham having a presence here, at last there is some stability.

At the same time that he was setting out Broadway and lining it in part with Birkin's warehouses, Hine was overseeing the erection of the magnificent and dignified warehouse for Messrs. Adams Page and Co. around the corner on Stoney Street. From starting design to completion took the architect about two and a half years. This impressive building, like an E in plan, varied between

The Birkin Building, Broadway, 1853-5. On the left a carriage is seen leaving the noted Birkin Gateway with its acknowledgement to client, architect and builder. (L.S.L.)

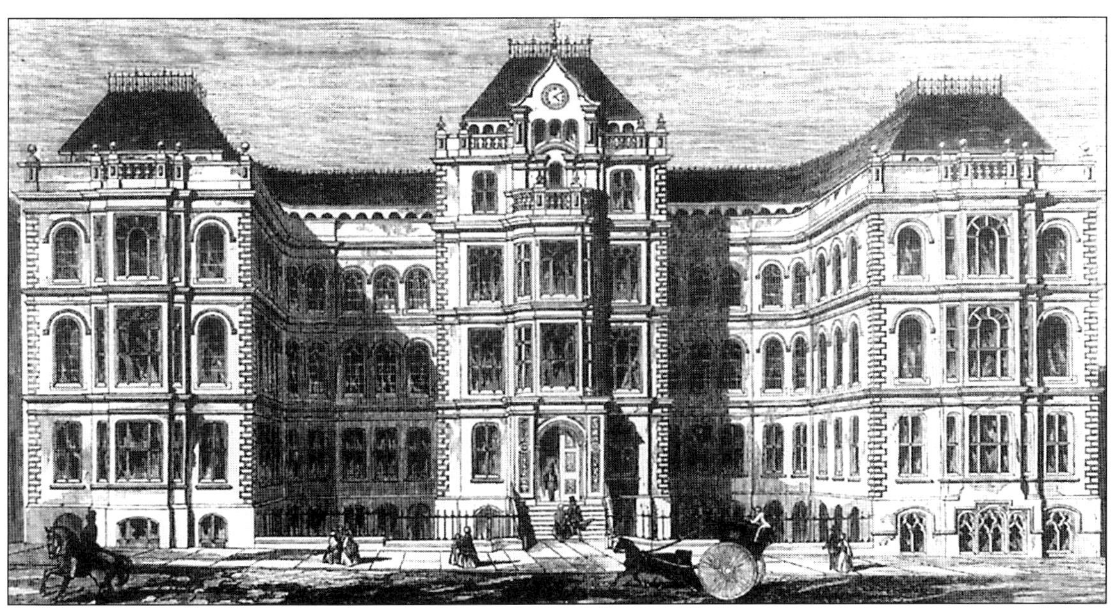

The Adams & Page warehouse, Stoney Street opened with a grand ceremony in July 1855. After years of decline massive investment has transformed the building into the city centre campus of New College Nottingham, now known as "Adams". (L.S.L.)

This warehouse, "Little Adams", was erected for Edward Steegman & Co. lace and hosiery manufacturers on Plumptre Street in 1861. The drawing was prepared in 1908 by the architects Sutton and Gregory prior to alterations. More recently the warehouse has been converted into apartments, "Stoneyard".

five and six storeys high. It had a frontage of 144 feet and a depth of 169 feet. The front entry was through doors with monogrammed wrought iron grilles at the top of a broad flight of steps leading to the first floor level. The rear entrance/exit opening onto St. Mary's Gate gave access centrally to a carriage court 80 feet by 35 feet.

Architecturally the warehouse was in Hine's Anglo-Italian style with the front laced with Ancaster and Derbyshire stone. The rear elevation on St. Mary's Gate was initially by comparison very plain. The extensions of about 1865, by which time Page had long been bought out, were more impressive. General working conditions were extremely good; roomy, well lit and, as required, heated by fresh warm air. "Worthy of emulation in every commercial establishment in the kingdom" stated a contemporary commendation. The spiritual welfare of the work force was catered for by the provision of both a chapel and a chaplain. Men and women had their own stairways. A separate building contained an employees' dining room, a men's tearoom and adequate washing facilities. The warehouse was opened with great ceremony on 10th July 1855. The festivities were reported at great length in the *Nottingham Review* of July 13 1855, and amidst the abundance of bonhomie, clients and employees, architect and builders, emerge with lavish praise and no little credit. The cost was estimated at approximately £15,000.

With the lace industry in decline in the 1920s and 1930s the Adams Company with its great warehouse had to diversify and take in tenants to survive. Among a number of these tenants was the firm of Cooper & Keywood, who arrived in 1933. When Thomas Adams was sold to S & J Watts in December 1958, Cooper and Keywood bought the building, in order to secure their future. By the early 1990s the physical state of the building was very poor due to rising repair costs, many floors being structurally weak. It had outdated standards of workspace and suffered from under occupation. In 1996 the building was acquired by the Lace Market Heritage Trust, and after extensive refurbishment at a cost of some £16.4 million is now the City Campus of New College Nottingham.

Hine had a good relationship with his builders, here it was Messrs Dennett with Messrs Fish dealing with the basement, and indeed an interesting aside to Hine's use of stone was a testimonial presented to him by a deputation of operative stonemasons on July 22nd, 1854. The address thanked him for introducing stonework to the extent he had done in his various designs and complimented him upon his high ability, taste and distinguished position. The testimonial consisted of "an exquisitely finished case of drawing instruments on top of which is a silver plate, bearing the inscription: 'Presented to T.C. Hine, Esq., Architect, by the Operative Masons of Nottingham, July 22nd, 1854'."

Hine used the opening of the Adams and Page warehouse to reply to the critics of his grand style and turned this criticism into an attack on the shabbiness of Nottingham's municipal buildings: "It has been said by some that it assumes too much importance for a lace warehouse and that it might be taken more for a town hall or an exchange. Now gentlemen . . . let me ask you whether it is the case that this building assumes more importance than it should do, or that the public buildings to which it is compared are less beautiful than they should be". [Referring to the Exchange, the predecessor of the Council House]. ". . . Standing as it does on perhaps the finest site, I was going to say in Europe, but certainly in England, I consider it a disgrace to us".

The Council took notice of Hine's outbursts and in 1857 the Town Improvement Committee issued a special invitation to him to submit designs for the "Improvement of Nottingham Market Place". Hine accepted the challenge enthusiastically, and soon the council was presented with plans for rebuilding the Exchange in the style of a grand French chateau and a formal layout for the Market Place. The Market Place was to be transformed into a sunken quadrangle lined by a series of arched covered stalls, set partly under the surrounding carriageways with grand flights of steps linking the two levels. A prominent insurance company was willing to finance the whole project in return for a 99-year lease of the ground floor at a nominal rent, but nothing happened.

When the town council seemed to be actively engaged in finding sites for new civic buildings in 1874-75 the topic was aired in the local press. Perhaps inevitably Hine was moved to write a long letter to the editor of the *Nottingham Journal*, dated May 4th, 1875. In the letter he restated his earlier proposals for " . . . the Exchange site . . . the grandest site in all England for a public

Hine's proposal for a new Exchange (1857). Would this design have answered the critics of the grandeur he gave to the Adams & Page warehouse - a mere building for the lace trade? Would the lowering of the central portion be capable of withstanding the demands of Nottingham in the C.21st century? (L.S.L.)

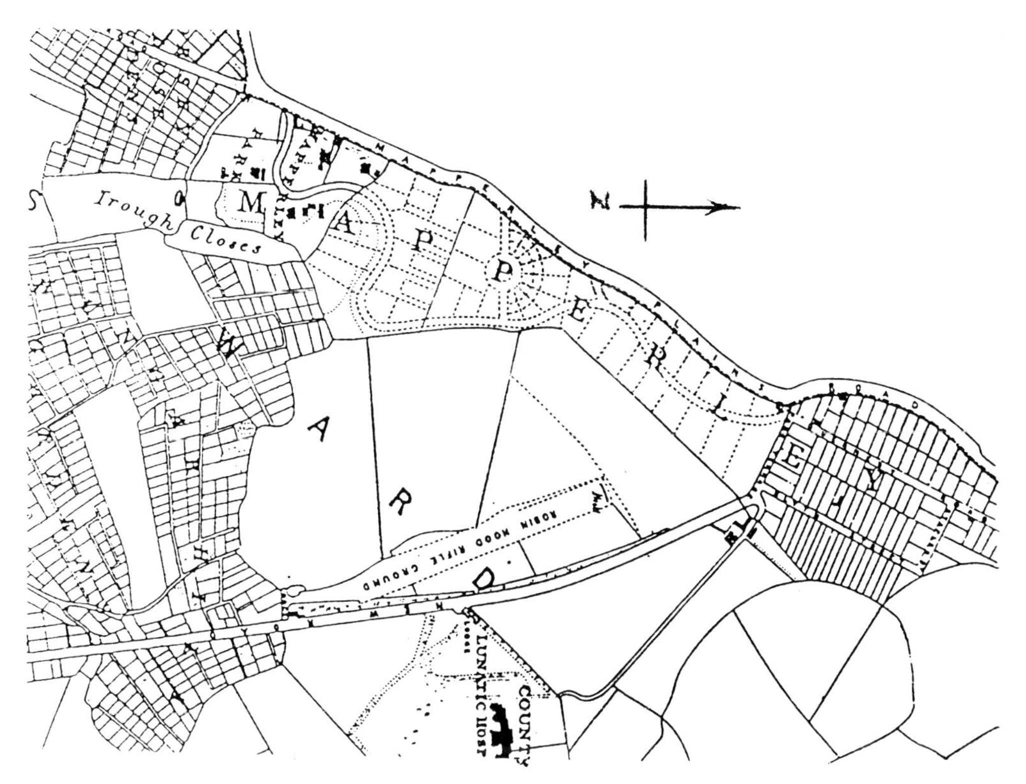

This portion of Jackson's Map of Nottingham, surveyed 1851-61 and published in 1861, shows Hine's tentative but unfulfilled proposals for the development of the Alexandra Park estate. Hine's four houses on or near The Crescent are shown; one can but speculate how the rest of the estate might have progressed.

building". "I may state briefly that they consisted of the formation of a street leading from St. Peter's Square into the Market Place, a continuation of the same into Parliament Street, the lowering of the central portion of the Market Place to a sufficient depth to allow an arcade for provision shops, &c., extending underneath the surrounding roadways, a large fountain in the centre and balustrade parapets and steps after the manner of those round Trafalgar Square in London, together with what possibly may have been a slight improvement upon the building which faces the latter in the shape of a new front to our Exchange."

However, this and later schemes for the rebuilding of the Exchange and restyling the Market Square were set aside for almost 70 years, when they involved another architect with the same initials, T. Cecil Howitt.

Although it is unlikely that many knew at the time, Thomas Adams & Co, supported by Hine, subsequently proposed a second road, through King's Place, connecting Stoney Street with St. Mary's Gate. The Corporation offered £300 but the idea was abandoned through lack of support from other owners.

In the autumn of 1853, just out of the Lace Market, Hine did cut a new street, Stanford Street, from Castle Gate down to Greyfriar Gate. Soon afterwards on its western side he produced warehouses for J. Lewis and Son (c.1854, now Stanford House) and at the junction with Greyfriar Gate for J. and H. Hadden and Co. Stanford (1854-55). This latter building, close to the present HMV store, was damaged when Zeppelins bombed the city in 1916. It was repaired but was demolished in the 1960s. Hine later recalled that on 30 November 1854 he suggested and cut "a new street through the old waterwheel buildings"- perhaps near the lower end of Finkhill Street.

Back in the Lace Market, Hine was the architect of the warehouse on Pilcher Gate-Halifax Place (c.1856) and of another for E. Steegman on Plumptre Street (1861). Both of these buildings have been converted into apartments. As noted already in 1865 he extended the warehouse of the successful Thomas Adams Company (late Adams and Page) on St Mary's Gate, taking the building around onto Warser Gate. An important group of factory buildings, the 'Meadow Mill' (c. 1865), was prepared for W. and F. Dobson on Queens Road: "The buildings have a highly ornamental facade of stone and dressed brick, and in every respect reflect credit on Mr. T.C. Hine, the architect".

Other industrial buildings by Hine dating from the 1850s and 1860s may survive. A warehouse on the eastern side of Maid Marian Way between Friar Lane and St. James's Street is just one for consideration.

The Birkin gateway, Broadway. The initials left to right are TCH Thomas Chambers Hine (architect), RB Richard Birkin (son), Bee motif, 1855, RB Richard Birkin (father), TB Thomas Isaac Birkin (son), G&H Garland and Holland (builders).

5. Quality Housing: The Park Estate, Alexandra Park and the Sandfield Area

After an unimaginative attempt to develop his Nottingham Park in 1822, the 4th Duke of Newcastle, as already noted, obtained the services of Peter Frederick Robinson in 1825. By May 1827 Robinson had prepared a development plan for the Park in the tradition of John Nash and was soon erecting his first houses on The Ropewalk and Park Terrace. Within five years, 40-60 had been completed but financial pressure and pique, following the burning of his Castle in October 1831, induced the Duke to invest elsewhere. This cessation of building was fortuitous, for Robinson's plan was seemingly oblivious of the topography of the Park. Attempting to impose a grid like street pattern on the area would have entailed earth movement of incredible magnitude.

However, c. 1839, just prior to the enclosure of the Derby Road-Lammas Fields area, No. 13 (demolished) 15 and 17-19 Park Valley and Lincoln Villa were built to Robinson's designs. These were intended both to test the market and to show prospective purchasers of the Park Estate its advantages over the building land in the town soon to be released through enclosure. The Duke's willingness to sell the whole estate at this time was, no doubt, influenced by his inability to finance its development, and also by the likelihood of the lowering of land values following the impending enclosure of first class housing land adjoining the estate. A tunnel, providing an impressive entry to the heart of the Park from Derby Road, was planned and work started on it early in 1844. The project was abruptly abandoned when more than half of the work had been completed. No architect/contractor for this project has been traced. In the late 1840s, with financial constraints lessened and the Park still in the Duke's possession, much of Western Terrace and Nos. 5, 7, 9, 11 and 21-23 Park Valley were built. Hine, not long out of his partnership with Patterson, has already been suggested as the most likely architect involved.

In 1851, the 4th Duke died and soon the 5th Duke decided to exploit the Park's unique possibilities as a prestigious estate. On 12th January 1854, Hine, now the best and busiest of the Nottingham architects, went to London to meet the architect Philip Hardwick, an advisor to the Duke of Newcastle. Before returning two days later he was offered and accepted the "Surveyship of the Park Estate" at a salary of £150 per annum. He now had a principal responsibility to plan and implement the future development of the Castle's former deer park. His proposals took well over 30 years to complete. Work started on "...the operation of cutting and paring the surface of portions of Nottingham Park...by means of the plough turf cutters..." on Wednesday 3rd February 1854. On 3rd July he set a local contractor Edwin Loverseed to recommence work on the Park Tunnel.

Around this time Robert Evans (1832-1911) entered Hine's office as a pupil*. Evans must have settled in quickly and impressed with his competence and maturity, for Hine delegated responsibility to him for managing the completion of the Park Tunnel. On the evening of 11th May 1855 young Robert, he was only 23, was in charge of the festivities at the *Milton's Head Hotel*, Derby Road, when the workmen engaged on the construction of the Park Tunnel celebrated the completion of the work. He "...complimented the workmen upon their general good behaviour, and expressed his satisfaction at their having arrived at this advanced stage of the works without any serious accident." The Park Tunnel consists of two distinct elements. The main tunnel from the Park side is about 240 feet long, 27 feet high and 23 feet wide cut from solid Bunter sandstone. College Street is spanned by a skew arch roughly the same height and width, finally a 33ft wide entrance roadway links the tunnel with Derby Road. The builders Hine used on the Birkin warehouses, Garland and Holland, were engaged for "Centering the Tunnel Arch" and as Loverseed's men did the excavating, Robert Evans had quite a mixed bunch to supervise.

Hine, assisted by Evans, devised and set out a geometrical plan for the Park based on two linked Circuses around which ran a series of crescents joined by parallel drives, which survive to this day. This layout is very close to that shown on Salmon's map of Nottingham dated 1861. Jackson's map of Nottingham published in the same year, but surveyed between 1851-61, is woefully inaccurate with respect to the Park, showing as it does signs of Robinson's grid pattern of 1827.

**Other pupils at various times in the 1850s included William Jolley, Laslett J. Pott R.A. R.B.A., Samuel Rollinson, and Mr Pegg.*

Hine's office was responsible for nearly 200 out of about 650 houses constructed in The Park. All other buildings put up in The Park during this time had to be approved by Hine as agent for the Duke of Newcastle. Several architects, in order to ensure approval, designed their houses in the style of Hine, some so successfully that it is now very difficult, visually, to distinguish a fake Hine. Hine's first houses in The Park in 1856 were the villas on Castle Grove with their Italian towers, shaped gables and classical doorways. Although he developed his most distinctive style by the 1860s, Hine built some of his grandest houses in the 1870s: Gothic and Elizabethan in Duke William Mount and the Italianate Peveril Tower. The Park Tunnel, given priority status in 1854, was intended as a direct route for carriages travelling between The Park and the town centre. However, the development of North Road as the main access road left the tunnel, as it remains today, a footpath into the heart of The Park. [For more about the Park refer to *The Park Estate*, Get To Know Nottingham Series].

In his old age Hine recalled many visits of the Duke(s) of Newcastle - mainly the 5th Duke - and two Park trustees W. E. Gladstone (a friend of the Duke's from their years at Oxford) and F. Ouvry to Nottingham to see at first hand how the development of the Park was progressing. The 5th Duke in many ways is a rather unfortunate figure. The commencement of work on the Park coincided with the outbreak of the Crimean war, and as Newcastle was Secretary of State for War he was responsible for turning a complacent peacetime army into a fighting fit expeditionary force and the logistics of transporting it to the Crimea. Long after it had ended, the war still left its mark on Newcastle and shortly after resigning as Colonial Secretary on the grounds of ill health he died suddenly at Clumber on 18th October 1864. It is little wonder, with more pressing demands on his mind early in 1854, that he agreed to start work on his prestigious estate on a modest budget of £10,000.

On August 23rd, 1853, Hine and his brother John purchased the Mapperley Hills Common, a little over 27 acres, for £5,946-12-0d. Almost immediately John bought his brother's rights to the land for £500 and purchased additional land for £2,858 making a total outlay of over £9,000. To pay for this, John Hine negotiated a loan of £5,800 on the understanding he spent £2,800 on erecting houses and £200 on forming and completing useful roads. A year later he raised a further £2,000 on a second loan. Unfortunately, by October 1855 he had failed to repay any money, loans or agreed interest. This would seem to be the root cause of the failure of the intended Alexandra Park Estate to materialise. The likely layout of what would have been an impressive estate, prepared by T.C. Hine, can be seen on Jackson's Map of Nottingham surveyed between 1851-61. The fact that simultaneously brother Thomas was successfully developing the Newcastle's Park Estate merely added to John's difficulties. Later there were problems with the family firm Hine and Mundella. Its main factory was destroyed by fire, rebuilt, and in 1864 the business was absorbed into the Nottingham Manufacturing Company. All of this gave John no respite. However, he appears to have honoured his original commitment, for his brother started laying out roads and by 1857 had commenced work on his four large houses. Fernleigh was built for William Windley, Springfield for brother Benjamin, Enderleigh for John (but never occupied by him; he had moved from Annesley Grove to London by 1862) and Sunnyholm, now Trent House. Benjamin remained at Springfield until c.1873. John held on to his undeveloped land west of Albert Road (south) and up to Ransom Road until around 1881 when he sold his holding to the town council.

Tantalisingly, contemporary accounts during the 1850s credit T. C. Hine with housing on the recently enclosed lands. This suggests on the new roads in the Sandfield area between the northern bounds of the old town and Forest Road. Stylistic evidence, that capricious mistress, abounds here but in the present absence of written evidence any deductions must be tentative. McIvor Terrace at the junction of Waverley Street and Forest Road West (c. 1865) and Rob Roy Terrace (mid 1870s) on the corner of Burns Street and Forest Road West show many details used by Hine on other buildings. Burns Street itself may contain more Hine buildings.

Two early styles from Hine's rich domestic repertoire to be seen in the Park Estate:

1. On Lenton Road on the southern side of the Park (c.1856),

2. On the northern boundary, Newcastle Drive, rear aspect (late 1850s).

Hine's earlier work at the former General Hospital; a third storey that was added to the old infirmary 1854-5, and a chapel of 1856. This idyllic scene has long disappeared. Multi-storey apartments now cover much of the foreground to the left and centre.

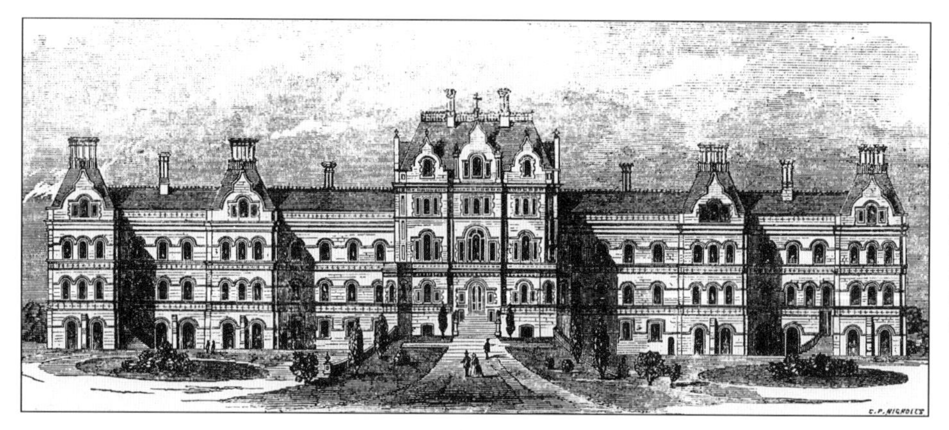

The former Coppice Hospital, Ransom Road, Mapperley (1857-9 and later), with its shaped gables, large mullioned windows and sweeping entrance provides a dramatic contrast to the austere Queen's Medical Centre. It has been refurbished and converted into apartments known as Hine Hall.

This photograph by Nottingham's pioneering photographer, Samuel Bourne, shows the Great Northern station, London Road, nearing completion in 1857. After years of indecision about its future it is now a popular health and fitness club, Holmes Place. (L.S.L.)

Hine in the Lace Market

The corner of Broadway and Stoney Street. Hine uses quoins here to give a strong vertical effect; very similar to the work he was carrying out at the same time, the mid 1850s, across the town in Regent Street. Broadway with its double curve was cut through the grounds of the old Plumptre House, linking Stoney Street with St. Mary's Gate.

"Adams", Stoney Street frontage. "Adams" the City Centre Campus of New College, Nottingham has been a leader in the revival of the fortunes of the Lace Market just as the Adams & Page warehouse was the catalyst for the establishment of a Lace Market identity when it opened with some splendour in July 1855.

The rear of the Adams building on St. Mary's Gate has much decorative detailing. Above the doorway to the right lace edging is cut in the stone. The four, eight pointed, stars may be considered Hine's mintmark. Here again Hine uses runs of quoins to telling effect. The cast iron portion of the largest doorframe can be seen. This is all part of the mid 1860s expansion of the warehouse.

Broadway was soon lined with warehouses, initially for Richard Birkin who had purchased Plumptre House in February 1853. Hine gave the warehouses he erected distinctive doorways; most of them survive largely unaltered. Two of these are illustrated above.

This Hine warehouse c.1856 can be seen on the corner of Halifax Place and Pilcher Gate. A variation of this bold window can be seen on a later Hine house in the Park Estate.

This is the surviving stained glass window of the pair, which long graced the chapel at the Adams warehouse. The chapel's Stoney Street door was replaced with a plain window during the building's recent refurbishment.

This French dome with its box finial, although somewhat irrelevant, caps Hine's westward extension of the Shire Hall, High Pavement, part of his refurbishment of the building after the calamitous fire of December 1876.

The original doors to the Adams & Page warehouse had a prominent A P in each of the wrought iron door panels.

Regent Street and Around

This view of the northern side of Regent Street stretches from Park Row (right) to the tree on the corner of Oxford Street. This must be one of Hine's greatest achievements.

Gables, Regent Street. Much of the northern side of Regent Street was built to Hine's designs in the 1850s; throughout the street there is an attractive display of shaped gables.

25 Regent Street, on the corner of Oxford Street, was the Hine family's home from 1846 until the architect's death in 1899.

This window with its simple geometrical stonework once illuminated Hine's drawing office at the family home, 25 Regent Street. The reflection is of 28/28A Regent Street, dated 1858.

No. 10 Oxford Street, a house of about 1859, clearly displays the reason why Hine was acclaimed for his revival of stone dressings on his buildings. Particularly noteworthy here is the tracery in the doorway and above the bay window.

28/28A Regent Street a Hine house of 1858, which has its main entrance on Oxford Street. It was later the first home of the Nottingham High School for Girls, prior to its move to Arboretum Street.

The Park Estate

This house on Castle Grove of about 1858 has a dramatic tower with lucarnes.

One of Hine's 1850s houses on Newcastle Drive, expansive on the Park side, more modest on the street side.

Another tower, this on 1 South Road, has very distinctive Italianate angled windows with corner columns. Variations of this style are present on other Park houses of the time, middle to late 1850s.

7 Newcastle Circus, a seasonal view of a fine house of the 1870s, this one in Hine's "mature classical" style.

19 Park Terrace, a late Hine house of 1881, is perched precipitously on the edge of the Park Tunnel. A terra cotta panel on the street frontage gives the date and the architects initials TCH.

1 Duke William Mount, located in the heart of the Park. This is another impressive house of the 1870s, with a side window remarkably like the Lace Market style of the 1850s.

Town and Around

County Club, Bridlesmith Gate and Bottle Lane 1869. Tile frieze incorporating **NC** and club motif.

The tall conservatory at Flintham Hall has a cast iron and glass barrel vault supported on hugely glazed but conventional walls. With a nominal date of 1853 the building has an impressive blend of Hine's Lace Market with Paxton's Crystal Palace.

Hine erected Gibson's hosiery warehouse about 1854 at the corner of Low Pavement and Lister Gate. It has been poorly refaced and in recent years has seen a variety of retail outlets in its divided ground floor.

Debenhams' Department Store, Market Street frontage (1872/1887). The opening of Market Street in 1865 gave R. and E. Dickinson, located on Long Row the opportunity to extend their store up the new street. The store later became Dickinson & Fazackerley, then Griffin & Spalding before becoming part of the Debenham group.

All Saints Church, Raleigh Street, was financed by the silk merchant, William Windley at total cost approaching £20,000. It was consecrated by the Bishop of Lincoln in 1864 in the presence of the Mayor and Corporation.

The former Bluecoat School, Mansfield Road, now the International Community Centre, was opened in July 1853. After some refurbishment the clock is working once again! The two statues of the traditionally dressed Bluecoat pupils, the boy can be seen, were the work of the stonemason John Stonehouse.

Hine's memorial in the Church Cemetery, before restoration.

The Hine memorial window in St. Mary's Church, High Pavement has the inscription "This window is dedicated by their children."

On Clarendon Street Hine built several houses, including Holly Mount about 1852 for his brother John. Later, around 1860, he designed the Clarendon Street School. Thomas, John and Benjamin Hine all purchased parts of land apportioned by the Enclosure Commissioners; eighteen plots in all. Of the seven bought by T.C. Hine, five were in the Meadows, the other two were in the Clarendon Street-Chaucer Street area.

In 1861 when a new lodge for Lenton Firs was planned, the tenant Thomas Adams appears to have asked Hine, architect of his Lace Market warehouse, to design the building. Lenton Firs Lodge survives on the Derby Road edge of the University campus.

6. Public Service: Hospitals and Stations

In 1854 Hine was invited by Thomas Birkin to prepare plans for enlarging the General Hospital by adding a third storey, and for erecting a hospital chapel between the main building and the fever house. The Bishop of Lincoln laid the foundation stone of the chapel on 24th October 1854. The work on the hospital was completed in 1855, increasing the number of beds to 136, and the Gothic style chapel in the following year. The chapel was long hemmed in by the expansion of the hospital; recent demolition work has revealed its modest charm. After redevelopment of the site it now provides office accommodation.

Thirteen years later, in 1869 Hine's daughter Mary purchased and presented No. 3 Postern Street to the committee formed to establish a hospital for sick and poor children. Her father duly carried out all architectural work needed to bring the hospital into commission. It opened on 1 July 1869. Work on a new accident wing for the General Hospital, which Hine intended to start in 1876, was delayed for archaeological reasons. The layout of the proposed works was such that it cut across the last visible parts of the old town wall and traces of the deep outer moat beyond. However, the antiquarian restrained the architect and the plan was modified. The foundation stone was finally laid on 28 March 1877 by Earl Manvers in the name of Countess Manvers. Decorative motifs used - "swags" in the then fashionable Queen Anne Revival may be seen in the Park Row elevation. [See 'Nottingham Hospitals', Get To Know Nottingham No. 4]

As a result of his commissions for the Birkin family, who had financial stakes in the evolving railway companies, Hine was appointed to build a series of stations for the Nottingham-Grantham line of the Great Northern Railway. The terminus for this line was erected at the Eastcroft at a cost of £20,000; known as the Great Northern Station, London Road, it opened in October 1857. It was also the headquarters of the Ambergate Company. By 1898 there were 71 daily passenger train arrivals but after the opening of the Victoria Station in 1900 the total declined to six. In 1944 the Low Level became a general goods and parcels station, converting to Nottingham Parcels Concentration Depôt in 1967. Finally in 1988 there was a complete closure of station, goods yard and sidings. Even before the sidings closed the station was the subject of various redevelopment proposals, most commendably as the hub of a comprehensive industrial museum for Nottingham. This, alas, never materialized, and after a period of dereliction the station has been well converted into a health and fitness centre. Meanwhile Hine's railway warehouse nearby is rotting away and desperately needs attention and investment. Hine was also responsible for the smaller stations on this line at Aslockton, Bingham, Orston (Elton & Orston) and Radcliffe-on-Trent.

In 1857-9 Hine designed the Coppice Hospital, the County Lunatic Asylum on Ransom Road, Mapperley. The Duke of Newcastle laid the foundation stone on 30 October 1857. Although neglected for some time after its closure, the building has been converted into a residential development "Hine Hall" with over 50 apartments. It has all the Hine characteristics: patterned brickwork, large mullioned windows and Elizabethan gables. Originally the hospital provided accommodation for 30 male and 30 female patients. A feature of the interior was the use of Hine's novel device for "Improvements in Lighting and Ventilation by Gas". This invention was patented, No. 545, in 1858.

No doubt as a result of all these commissions Hine took his former pupil, Robert Evans, into partnership some time during 1857 and in the following year his eldest son, George Thomas, became an articled pupil.

7. Church Architect in Town and County

In 1864 the Bishop of Lincoln, accompanied by the Mayor and Corporation, consecrated the new church of All Saints, Raleigh Street. This impressive Gothic church, with its schools and parsonage forming one unified group of buildings, was designed by Hine and Evans and financed by William Windley, a silk throwster, at a total cost of around £20,000. The 75 feet Lincolnshire broach spire on a 100 feet tower, and an elaborate polygonal apse in the French Gothic style, give distinction to a beautifully simple building. The interior, heated by hot water pipes, was graced by a font of red Mansfield stone and a circular pulpit of Caen stone ornamented with alabaster and marble. Taylor of Loughborough supplied a peal of eight bells. An attractively refurbished terrace of houses, nearby on All Saints Street, would appear to be by Hine.

All Saints was only one of a number of local and county churches designed by Hine. Earlier in 1856, on a site given by the Duke of Newcastle, Hine built one of his suburban churches, Christ Church, Cinderhill. For £2,000 he produced a decorated Gothic church with, in the southwest, an octagonal turret surmounted by a small spire. Carved heads of the sovereigns, still well preserved, decorate the exterior and form corbels in the interior of the church.

Hine (between 1857-67 Hine and Evans), was responsible for altering and adapting - "restoring" - a number of county churches. Many Victorian architects over-restored, as did Hine in 1859, when he laid hands on St. Michael's Church, Laxton, a fine large building, too big for the parish to keep in good order. He dismantled and rebuilt the tower further east, thus shortening the nave and destroying the proportions of the ancient building. Nevertheless, other commissions for churches followed. St. Michael's, Farnsfield, (1859-60); the colliers' church, St. Luke's at Shireoaks, (1861-3) for which H.R.H. the Prince of Wales laid the foundation stone, and the elaborate unfinished chapel at Clumber House for the 5th, ultimately the 6th, Duke of Newcastle (1864). Hine had gone to Clumber as early as 19 March 1856 to discuss a domestic chapel. The 6th Duke was allegedly too financially embarrassed to ensure its completion. This chapel at Clumber was demolished by the 7th Duke, probably making it Hine's shortest lived building, and replaced by the present chapel by Bodley and Garner (1886-9).

In St. Matthias' Church, Carlton Road, Sneinton, (1867) Hine achieved the most striking results at the minimum of cost. A severely simple exterior was in contrast to the "beautiful and devotional" interior. A lofty nave has Bulwell stonewalls lined with red brick with black brick bands and panelling. The eastern end has a circular apse whilst the west gable is surmounted by a high bellcote. For £3,000 Hine managed to provide 700 sittings.

A church with a very short life span was St. Stephen's, Bunker Hill, off Parliament Street. It was the Trinity Free Church of 1859, and enlarged to Hine's designs in 1869. The original church was "not an attractive edifice". It was so dark, being closely hemmed in by tall buildings, that Hine put windows in the roof to let in more light. The whole area was cleared in 1897 to make way for Victoria Station.

Other churches in the county were restored by Hine: St. George, Barton-in-Fabis, (1855 and 77), St. Margaret, Bilsthorpe, (1873), St. Giles, Darlton, (1855), St. Oswald, Dunham-on-Trent, (1861-2), St. Lawrence, Gonalston, (1853), St. Edmund, Holme Pierrepont, (1878-81), All Saints, Ordsall, (1876), Priory Church of St. Peter, Thurgarton, (1852-3), and part of St. Giles, West Bridgford, (1872). He also built a number of rectories and in Nottingham, the Elizabethan style Convent of the Sisters of St. Joseph, off Mapperley Road, (1875). His last church alteration in Nottingham was in 1874 when the 'Free and Independent' Methodist Chapel in Park Row was converted into an Episcopal Church, St. Thomas's, demolished in 1931. The site now forms part of the Albert Hall redevelopment. In 1863 Hine and Evans received the first prize of £20 in the open competition for St. Ann's Church, Wells Road, Nottingham. However, when it was built in 1864 it was to the designs of Robert Clarke of Nottingham.

Christ Church, Cinderhill, built by Hine in 1856 on land given by the 5th Duke of Newcastle. (Illustrated London News, L.S.L.)

Hine's drawing of St. Lawrence, Gonalston, which he rebuilt in 1853 (N.R.O.).

The architect's drawing of the Church, School and Parsonage of All Saints, Raleigh Street, Nottingham. The spire still dominates the skyline from the Arboretum area. Hine was often engaged in building or restoring churches. In October 1871 he was appointed Diocesan Surveyor for the County of Nottingham.
(Reproduced by permission of the P.C.C. of All Saints Church).

8. Hine At Large

In 1865 Sheep Lane was widened and renamed Market Street. The existing Long Row premises of R. and E. Dickinson and Fazackerley (later Fazackerley, Griffin and Spalding, and currently Debenhams), located alongside this work, were now on a valuable corner site. The store was rebuilt and extended up the eastern side of Market Street by Hine and Evans. In digging out the foundations for the new store, Hine again found caves cut below other caves in the underlying Bunter sandstone. Although the Long Row frontage has been altered at least twice, Hine's original work, with distinctive window surrounds, survives on Market Street. Now at last he had one of his buildings near the heart of the town, but he had received little recognition outside the Midlands.

Hine's biggest commission outside the county had been the large country house, Cranfield Court in Bedfordshire, built for the Reverend G.C. Harter (1862-4). Harter was, like Thomas Birkin, a director of the Great Northern Railway and as befitted his position, Hine built him a grand house in the Italianate style with Gothic and Romanesque embellishments. At Cranfield, Hine also built the school and restored the church.

The Butter Cross, in the Market Square, Bingham, erected in 1861 as a memorial John Hassell of Shelford Manor, agent to the Earl of Chesterfield, is attributed to Hine.

In Lincolnshire, Hine was responsible for All Saints, Broxholme, (1857), St. Peter's, Aisthorpe, (1867), and the truly Victorian Old Rectory at Beelsby, (1868). Hine and Son restored St. Michael's, Coningsby, (1870).

In Derbyshire Hine was the architect of a number of churches: Morton Holy Cross Church (1850), St. Paul, Hasland, Chesterfield, (1850-1), Holy Trinity Church and Parsonage, Brackenfield, (1850) and Victoria Street Chapel, Derby, (1860s). At St. Martin's Church, Alfreton, (1868) he carried out alterations and additions. Foston Hall, Scropton, is a Hine Jacobean house of 1863. It is likely that Hine went back to the Grammar School in Chesterfield for extensions in 1860 and 1862. He certainly served as Architectural Assessor for the competition for Chesterfield Public Hall in 1874.

An amusing incident, no doubt considered seriously by Hine, occurred when he took his family to Filey for a holiday lasting from 16 July to 13 August 1858. Mr. Pegg, one of his architectural assistants, called on him. As Hine recalled "Met Mr. Pegg and made designs of Ormanston Road, Chapel (Derby) on the sands with my walking stick and subsequently carried it into execution."

Hine and Evans were responsible for the chancel at St. Werburgh, Hanbury, Staffordshire (1862), which was possibly their only work in that county.

Hine and Son were unsuccessful entrants in competitions for a Baptist Church in Sheffield, (1869) and the restoration of Matlock Church (1870).

In 1865 Hine, then 52 had his last chance to become a nationally known architect. Although not on the original list invited to enter the competition for the design of St. Pancras Station and Midland Grand Hotel, he was one of the three architects later added to complete the list of ten competitors. No doubt Richard Birkin's influence as a director of the Midland Railway and Hine's work for the Great Northern, justified his nomination. The design submitted by Hine and Evans was estimated to cost £255,000 to build. George Gilbert Scott's winning design, initially estimated at £316,000, was altered and extended so as finally to amount to nearly £1,000,000. Sad to relate, Hine and Evans were not placed in the first four in order of merit. Little other than the winning design remains of this competition.

Another open competition in 1866 in Nottingham was for new premises on Arboretum Street for the Free Grammar School, now Nottingham High School [for Boys.] The winning entries failed to impress the judges and Thomas Simpson, a prominent local architect and member of the Town Council, was invited to prepare a scheme. Simpson accepted and soon involved Hine and Evans as assistants on the design and construction of the new school.

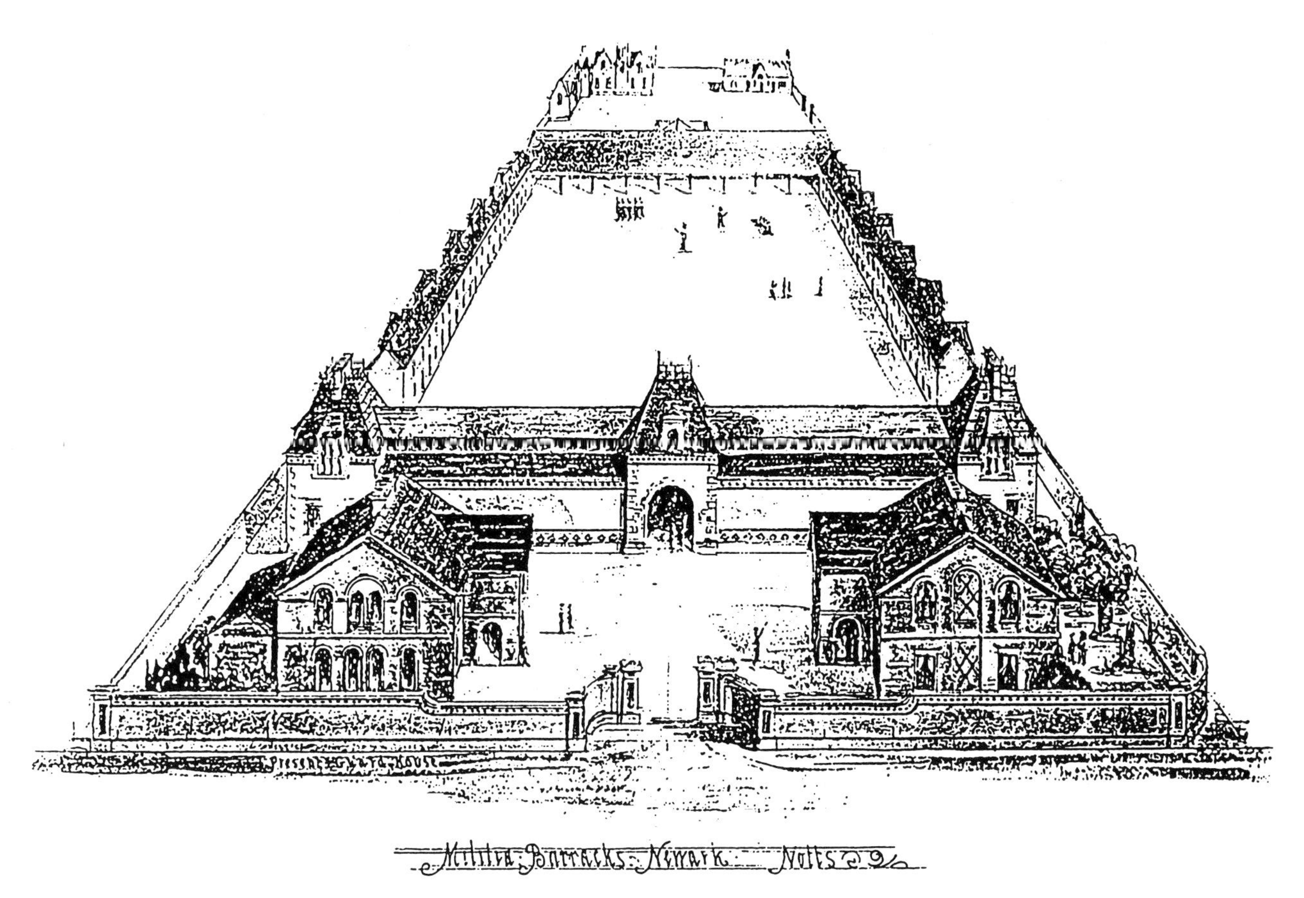

After Hine reported on the defective state of the Militia Storerooms at Newark in 1861, he prepared this unexecuted design for new Barracks at Newark (1862). (N.R.O.)

Cranfield Court, Bedfordshire (1862–4) was Hine's largest project out of Nottinghamshire. Here many of the facets of the architect's earliest style are brought together. Shaped gables, classical windows, balconies, clustered chimneys, quoins, diapering, bands of buff tiles and, of course the obligatory tower with 'beheaded' spire and lucarnes overpower the simplicity of the service wing to the right. Sadly the house was demolished in the 1930s although a lodge survives. Hine incorporated an early form of double-glazing in his design. All windows in the principal rooms were formed of double sheets of quality glass. In some cases sunblinds were placed between the panes.

A major project for Hine and Evans, for which extensive plans were prepared but never implemented, was the rebuilding of the Militia Barracks at Newark, (1862). This assignment followed Hine's report, prepared for the County Justices, on the defective state of the Militia Store Rooms in 1861.

On May 9th, 1864, the new reservoir on Robin Hood Chase was opened. Measuring 220 feet by 133 feet; holding 2.5 million gallons; covering 1.5 acres and costing £3,000, this was an important undertaking. The design was by Hine and the work carried out by Loverseed, the contractor he used in laying out the Park Estate.

In 'Village and Cottage Architecture: Select Examples of Country and Suburban Residences Recently Erected' published by Blackie and Son in 1868, Hine and Evans were represented by two villas. One was on the eastern side of Grantham whilst the other, one of a pair, was opposite the Baptist Chapel in Osmaston Road, Derby. Both were dated 1864.

After Robert Evans left the partnership early in 1867, Hine took his son, George Thomas, as a partner on 4 August of that year. The first notable venture of T.C. Hine and Son was the County Club at the junction of Victoria Street/Bridlesmith Gate and Bottle Lane, which opened in 1869. In a letter written about 1868 the contractor John Loverseed records that whilst excavating the foundations of the club on Bottle Lane he found an original street or track about 11 feet down.

Feeling the need for new offices for the new partnership in September 1871 Hine purchased land for £701 adjoining the County Club premises. Building plans were submitted the following month and father and son moved into their new offices, at 2 Victoria Street, in 1872. A feature of the façade of this five-storey building was a line of eight of the architect's decorative leitmotif: eight-pointed stars in concentric moulded circles. The family home remained in Regent Street.

The County Club, much altered at ground floor level, now houses travel agents, with solicitors above. Alas, the distinctive Hine tower on its corner has long been removed, but the original 'string' of decorative tiles displaying the club motif and the entwined letters **N.C.** (Nottinghamshire Club) survives. Hine's office disappeared in 1920-1 when the Midland Bank's premises were extended.

In October 1871 Hine was appointed Diocesan Surveyor at Lincoln and in 1885 he became one of the six Surveyors of Ecclesiastical Dilapidations for the Diocese of Lincoln

9. The Castle and the Courts

The blackened burnt out shell of Nottingham Castle had provided a sombre backdrop to the development of the Park Estate. The Castle had been set on fire by Reform Bill rioters in October 1831, and after the minimum of clearing up, had, in effect, been left to the ravages of the elements during the lifetime of the Fourth Duke. There was the possibility that the Fifth Duke, prompted by Hine who enthused over the Castle's past glories, would initiate some restoration.

Hine in fact later recounted that "the possibility of some day restoring the Castle as an occasional residence was ever a favourite theme" with the 5th Duke of Newcastle. On one occasion, after he had escorted the Duke and Lord Overstone around the Castle site and whilst discussing its potential over a glass of sherry, Lord Overstone proposed "And now we will drink success to the *New Castle*." Alas nothing happened.

After the Duke's death in 1864, various schemes were put to the new Sixth Duke for the smoke stained ruin of the Castle. Hine was a consultant and advisor on these proposals. However, when Hine presented the Duke with a proposal made by the County Magistrates for converting the Castle into a prison and Court of Justice, he was asked if he thought his father would have consented to such a scheme, had he been alive. Hine replied: "No, sir, honestly speaking I do not think he would". To which the young Duke replied: "I will not give it mine". Another suggestion was to convert the Castle into military barracks.

In 1872 Hine and Son moved into their new office at 2 Victoria Street. This office, with its decorative run of eight roundels each with an eight pointed star, was lost in 1920-1 when the adjoining premises of the Midland Bank were extended. An indistinct figurehead appears at the base of the tourelle. Prior to moving into this office Hine's practice was in the family home, 25 Regent Street. The eight-pointed star motif appears so often on Hine's buildings it could be considered his leitmotif. (N.R.O.)

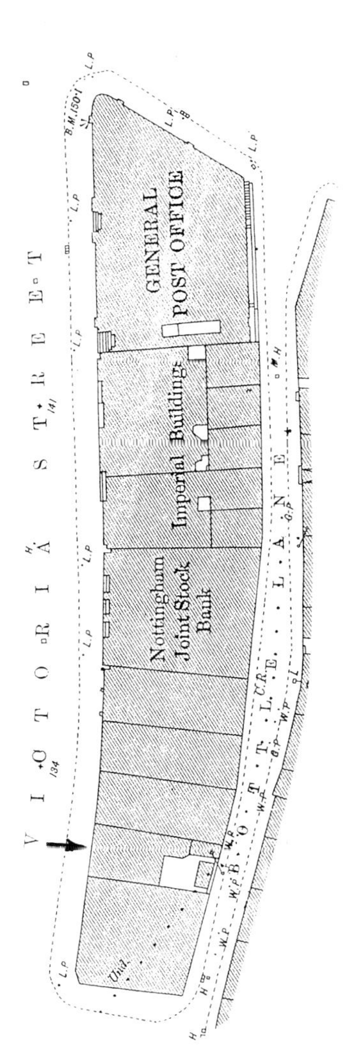

The Greyfriar Gate premises of J. and H. Hadden and Co., designed by Hine c.1854, were damaged during the raid by Zeppelin L17 on 23rd September 1916. Although repaired under the direction of E.R. Sutton early in 1917, the building has long been demolished. It was another example of the architect's 1850s warehouse style. (L.S.L.)

The choice of the Castle as a site for a provincial museum of art was the climax of a sequence of events, which started in 1872. On 19 January in that year Sir Henry Cole K.C.B., then Director of the South Kensington Museum, wrote to the Mayor of Nottingham, W.G. Ward, offering some suggestions about the possibility of establishing a museum in Nottingham closely connected with that at South Kensington. The basis of this proposition was to build on the high esteem, which the Nottingham School of Art had acquired nationally. The South Kensington Museum would deliver "a continuous supply of suitable objects to a Science and Art Museum at Nottingham", if the town would only make the proper responsible arrangements for their reception and safe custody. Each year the Council would receive a different selection of material from the South Kensington collections for their exhibition.

The onus was now with the town, and a tenuous search for a site suitable for a permanent museum commenced. The initial move to follow up Sir Henry's offer was to set up an exhibition in the Exchange Hall; this meant sacrificing the only large room in the possession of the Council, not an unopposed move! The exhibition contained over 800 objects on loan from South Kensington together with considerable private loans. The exhibition opened in May 1872 and it was at its inauguration that the first public mention was made of what became popularly known as the Castle scheme. Hine, who happened to be at that meeting, spoke enthusiastically in support, pointing out that as the local custodian of the Castle he had been previously authorised by the trustees of the Park Estate to take into consideration the best means of utilising the structure. He had prepared plans with the view of converting it into dwelling houses; transforming it into a Museum seemed however a much grander and more worthy idea. He promised to support an application from the town for such an appropriation of the building, and to use his best endeavours to obtain it for that purpose on reasonable terms. Writing later, Hine modestly pointed out that he had informally suggested the use of the Castle "some time previously".

At the meeting of the Town Council held on 4 August 1873 the School of Art and Exhibition Committee submitted a report on the undoubted success of the South Kensington loan exhibition, including the plea "that before long some steps will be taken to acquire for the Exhibition a home commensurate with its importance." Later at the same meeting the Museum Site Committee recommended the acquisition of the Castle and Grounds from the Trustees of the late Duke of Newcastle, to house the Art Exhibition and Museum.

The question of funding the acquisition was raised at the Council meeting held on 16 October 1873. Further moves were also on the agenda. Powers to bring about the acquisition would be sought in the forthcoming (1874) Nottingham Improvement Bill, and the Museum Committee was authorized to negotiate with the Newcastle Trustees to acquire the site either in fee or for not less than 500 years, and to open a subscription list. This subscription list met with public approval and within two years £10,000 was promised.

On May 10 1875, the first meeting between the Trustees and the Mayor and influential men of the town took place at the Drill Hall at the Castle. As a result, the Castle and the major part of its grounds were leased to the town for a term of 500 years for "Purposes connected with the advancement of Literature, Science, and Art, the education, recreation, and general good of the inhabitants of Nottingham and neighbourhood." Full details were given to the Council on 30 September, and the Mayor, William Lambert, signed the lease on October 11th, 1875.

Hine and Son were the only architectural practice invited to prepare plans for the adaptation of the "blackened ruin" into the "Midland Counties Museum and Gallery of Art." The Museum Committee pointed out that Messrs Hine and Son had taken a very great interest in the Castle scheme, and as they were acting as Surveyors to the Duke of Newcastle's Trustees, under the provisions of the lease, would have "to pass all plans, by whomsoever designed, relative to any work executed at the Castle."

Fortunately the Council approved the designs submitted by Hine and Son on 17 January 1876 and so between the years 1876-8 Hine carried out his labour of love, converting the gutted shell of the Renaissance palace into the first provincial Museum of Fine Art. The estimate was for the building conversion was £21,200. However the total cost inclusive of landscaping but exclusive of furniture was about £27,000. The shell of the building had suffered comparatively little from the fire of 1831,

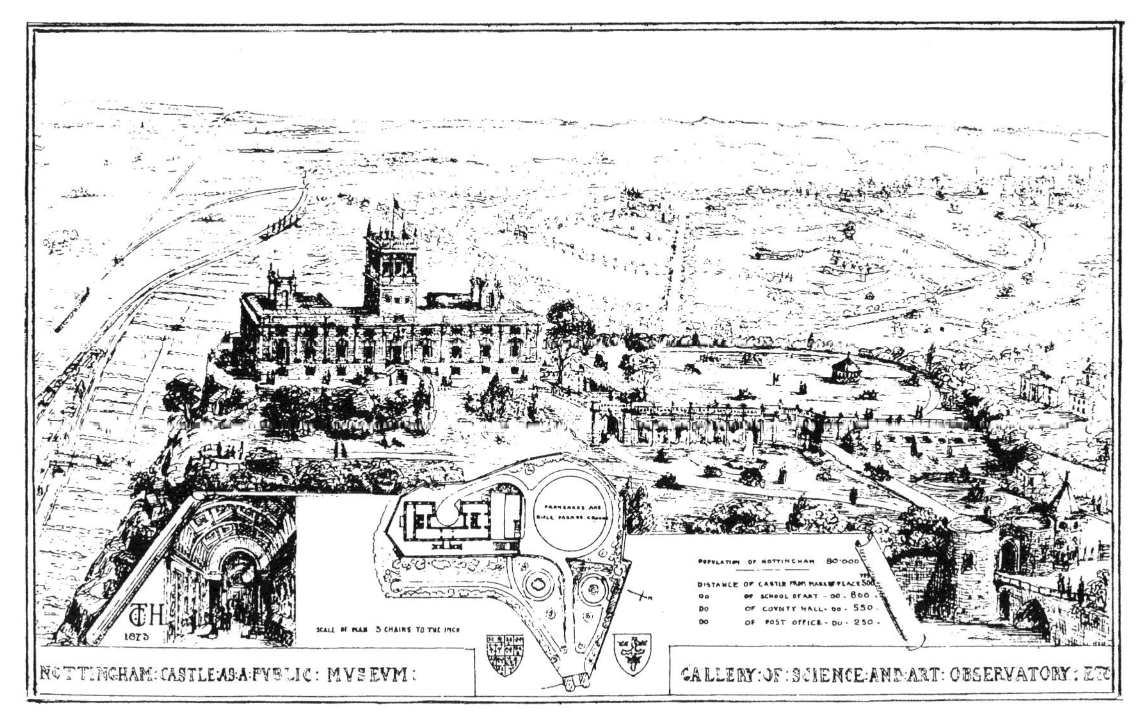

Hine prepared this plan for the restoration of the blackened ruin of Nottingham Castle in 1873 when the idea of a possible future use of the building as a museum was first proposed. This was almost three years before the Town Council approved Hine & Son's more modest designs for converting the Castle into a Museum of Fine Art. (L.S.L.).

This is Hine's drawing of the Nisi Prius or Civil Court at the Shire Hall, Nottingham, which he restored and enlarged between 1877-9 after extensive fire damage.
(The Architect 22 February 1879, N.R.O.).

The Ilkeston Road Board School was one of several projects undertaken by George Thomas Hine whilst in partnership with his father. It became more familiar as the "Radford Boulevard Schools". It now houses several social initiatives.
(The Building News, 23 September 1887, L.S.L.).

but all the woodwork of the mansion, floors and staircases, had gone. The new staircase was of stone with a cast iron balustrade and for the formation of galleries two storeys, the lower of 18 feet and the upper of 23 feet, replaced the three storeys of the Ducal Palace. This meant that the new floors cut across the windows of the old staterooms.

The Midland Counties' Art Museum at Nottingham Castle was opened by the Prince of Wales, later King Edward VII, on July 3rd, 1878, and the whole town was en fête for the day. When the Prince and Princess Alexandra inspected the interior of museum, Mr. Hine and Mr. Wallis, the Museum's curator, acted as guides.

Reacting quickly to Sir Henry Cole's challenge of 1872, Hine had prepared a design for the Castle in 1873, adding an Italianate observatory tower to the centre of the building. Possibly on financial grounds or lack of civic interest, this remained his dream.

Another prestigious public work, undertaken by Hine between 1877-79, was the rebuilding and enlargement of the Shire Hall, Nottingham. After a disastrous fire, which broke out on December 1st, 1876, little remained of the interior of Gandon's building of 1770 and W. Bliss Sanders' recently completed eastern wing of 1874-6. The facade on High Pavement and the Grand Jury Room did survive. Insurance cover of £4,000 allowed restoration of the Crown Court to start immediately. A further £5,000 was raised by the County Authorities to enable the reconstruction of the entrance hall and an overdue enlargement of the much-criticised Nisi Prius Court to take place at the same time. The Visiting Justices directed that provisional estimates be prepared but no indication why Hine and Son were chosen as preferred architects has been uncovered. Perhaps the Insurers made the selection; perhaps the architects' work on the fire-damaged Castle, then currently in progress, suggested a logical choice. Certainly there was some urgency to bring the courts back into use as soon as possible.

Hine's obsession with Italianate detailing ruined Gandon's essentially simple design. On the façade there were originally six plain niches, Hine replaced four niches with doorways framed by prominent moulding and surmounted by a heavy triangular pediment. He inserted round-headed windows into the other two. Other parts of the frontage were similarly 'enhanced'. Hine used a variation of his Italianate interpretation for the exterior of the extended Nisi Prius Court, the whole being beneath an irrelevant French dome. The interiors of the courts do have a distinct charm and acoustically were an improvement on Gandon. A massive shaped pediment on which was carved the Royal Arms was placed above the main entrance. Thankfully, this was removed in June 1932. The Shire Hall was empty and unwanted for several years after the Courts were transferred elsewhere, but eventually the building was transformed into an important educational resource and tourist attraction "The Galleries of Justice", which opened in April 1995.

10. Friendships

In October 1859 Marriott Ogle Tarbotton (1834-87) was appointed Nottingham's first full time Borough Surveyor and Engineer. He was in modern terminology a 'workaholic'. Although not yet 25 when he came to Nottingham he quickly immersed himself in the problems of the old town and the failings of the New Nottingham created as a result of the passing of the 1845 Enclosure Act. Drainage, sewerage, water and gas supply, and an occasional flourish of architecture all came within his orbit.

Tarbotton developed a strong friendship with Hine, possibly begun and developed through their working relationship. Hine, in a journal compiled later in life recorded some of their joint ventures. On 6 October 1864 they travelled together to Leamington, then on to Bath and elsewhere to examine sewage disposal. In 1869 Hine noted "Self and M. O. Tarbotton to Venice etc." In November 1873 he took a 17-day trip on the Continent with Tarbotton. On 12 July 1875 they travelled with the Town Clerk to London, where they dined with A. J. Mundella, who was now an MP. From 3-8 October 1878 they accompanied the Castle Committee on a visit to Paris.

It is likely that Hine helped Tarbotton find a good house in the Park Estate when he moved there from Newstead Grove in the early 1870s. Hine no doubt used the friendship to help ensure a part of the old Trent Bridge was saved from demolition after the new bridge, built to Tarbotton's design, opened on 25 July 1871. Hine's intervention ensured that two arches at the southern end of the ancient bridge were preserved. They are still there, incongruously hidden in a traffic island. It is possible that the two friends discussed, informally, the location and the architecture of the new Guildhall and the University College/Library block, which included provision for a museum.

Starting in 1883, the state of Tarbotton's health increasingly gave cause for concern. He still carried a heavy workload, and was taken home partially paralysed on Friday 4 March 1887 from a meeting of the Sewage Farm Committee. The next day he rallied and tried to carry on working, following a relapse however, he died on Sunday evening 6 March. Three days later at his funeral at the Church Cemetery the carriage of his friend T. C. Hine was one of several that followed the hearse.

The eminent Liberal politician William Ewart Gladstone, on his visits to Nottingham as a trustee of the Park Estate, always called on Hine. Hine recalled one particular meeting: "9 December 1867 W.E. Gladstone and F. Ouvry agreed to the formation of Pleasure Grounds in the Park. Lunched with them at the George (Hotel)." Another visit achieved a short report in the Nottingham Daily Express 5 December 1867. "VISIT OF MR GLADSTONE TO NOTTINGHAM - On Tuesday morning last, Mr. Gladstone, who had arrived in Nottingham the previous evening, in company with Mr. Ouvry and Mr. T.C. Hine visited the warehouses of Messrs. Thomas Adams and Company, Stoney Street, and the Nottingham Manufacturing Company, Station Street. On returning, the party inspected the alterations in St. Mary's Church, and then walked through the Park, to see the improvements, which are being carried out on this portion of the late Duke of Newcastle's estate, of which the right hon. gentleman is trustee. At noon Mr. Gladstone lunched at Mr. Hine's Regent Street, the Mayor and Town Clerk being invited to meet him. The right hon. gentleman, whose business was strictly private, left Nottingham by the three o'clock train." Hine was also present on that well-remembered occasion, 11 May 1875, when the sixty six year old Gladstone cut down a tree in the Park, a section from the tree was suitably mounted, inscribed and displayed on Tunnel Road in the Park Estate until relatively recently.

Another great friend was William Stevenson (1832-1922), a businessman but also an enthusiastic and knowledgeable local historian who was always modestly respectful of his friend's seniority. He later became a Vice-President of the Thoroton Society. Hine helped to persuade the Town Clerk to employ Stevenson's eldest son William Henry, a fine scholar, to edit the Borough Records. He edited the first four volumes, before being elected to a research fellowship at Exeter College, Oxford.

11. Professional and Antiquarian

Hine never joined the Institute of British Architects but in November 1862 did help set up the Nottingham Architectural Association "to promote unity among its members, the establishment of uniformity of practice and for the general promotion of the profession of architecture". Initially he was vice president and chairman of the Committee of Management. In the following year he succeeded Henry Moses Wood as president, a post he held continuously for ten years. His successor as president was his former partner Robert Evans. His son, George Thomas Hine, was a fellow of the R.I.B.A. This fellowship entitled him to a place on the R.I.B.A. Council 1888-89 whilst serving as president of the N.A.A.1888-90.

Earlier, when George applied for the post of Surveyor of the County of Nottingham in 1879, he was supported by the current president of the R.I.B.A., Charles Barry, who wrote to T. C. praising George and adding "...like yourself zealous, hardworking and well able to discharge with efficiency any undertaking he takes in hand". Unfortunately George was unsuccessful, Edwin Parry, M.I.C.E. of Nottingham being appointed to the post on a salary of £300 p.a.

The Hine family was associated with the Robin Hood Rifles from its inception in 1859. The first six volunteers included Hine's son George, his young partner Robert Evans, and A.J. Mundella of Hine and Mundella. Hine, as the Duke of Newcastle's agent, was asked for permission to hold a parade in the Castle grounds. Naturally he readily approved and the intrepid six received their first drill on the Castle terrace during the evening of Saturday May 28th 1859. Hine in fact removed a flight

This photograph of T.C. Hine and W.E. Gladstone, right, discussing plans for the restoration of the Castle was superimposed on a photograph of the ruined 'shell'.

"The Mayor of Nottingham receiving from the architect (Hine) the key of the Midland Counties Art Museum, and presenting the same to the Prince of Wales."

(Original in The Graphic)

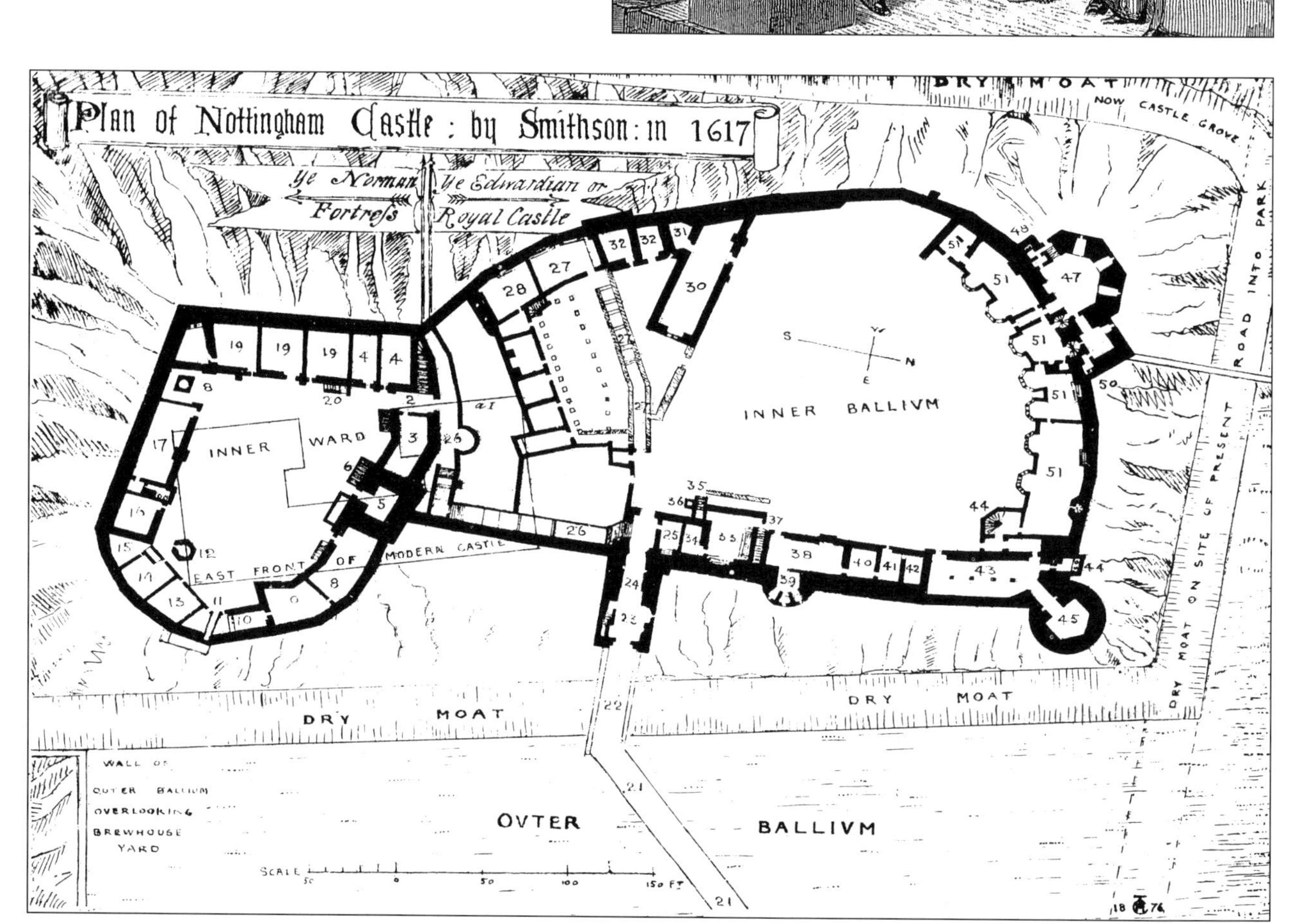

Hine's redrawing, dated 1876, of Robert Smythson's Plan of Nottingham Castle 1617. No doubt this drawing was part of his restoration strategy. (All L.S.L.).

of steps from the Castle to improve this "parade ground", a move he later regretted. Hine was soon involved in designing the insignia for the corps's uniform.

The Queen Anne's Bowling Club was founded on 15th April 1856. T.C. Hine was a founder member and no doubt helped to arrange the lease to the club of its first green near the Park-side entrance to the Park Tunnel. The rent was fixed at one guinea per annum for 30 years from 1856. Ten years later Hine was probably instrumental in organizing the club's move to its present location, higher up on Duke William Mount at the heart of the Park, in 1867.

Starting in the 1860s Hine emerged as a respected lecturer. In 1864 he spoke on the archaeology of Nottingham Castle to the Lincoln Diocesan Architectural Society meeting in Nottingham. In the same year, at a meeting of the Nottingham Architectural Association, he gave a paper on the 'Architecture of Italy' which he illustrated ". . . with some large photographs which were studiously examined and admired". At least one of his later occasional papers, 'Warming and Ventilation', delivered to the N.A.A during the session of 1874 was issued as a pamphlet. His most important address, entitled 'The Raising of the Standard of War by King Charles I at Nottingham in 1642', was given to the British Association meeting at Nottingham in 1866. Thereafter he did, from time to time, talk to a variety of audiences particularly on the Castle or St. Mary's Church. Although he was associated with St. Mary's Church in his later years, he was in 1846 a churchwarden at St. Nicholas's Church. He was a founder member of the Nottingham Literary and Philosophical Society and exhibited photographs at their conversaziones in October 1870 and 1871.

Hine had several heroes, of these Charles I, and William Cavendish, the 1st Duke of Newcastle were well known. Less celebrated was William Stretton (1755-1828), a former architect and surveyor to the Nottingham Corporation and the Duke of Newcastle. Stretton, a keen local historian and archaeologist, had prepared manuscript notes for an intended History of Nottingham. These notes came into Hine's possession and no doubt influenced his writing of that bizarre compendium of Nottingham's history entitled 'Nottingham Its Castle, A Military Fortress, A Royal Palace, A Ducal Mansion, A Blackened Ruin, A Museum and Gallery of Art'. The first edition was published in 1876 and a second edition, with a supplement covering the formal opening of the new museum, was published in 1879, price 12/6d (= 62·5p).

Generally the book was well received at the time, but it is factually inaccurate. The reviews were mixed. *The Saturday Review* 23 October 1880 whimsically observed "Altogether it is quite the style of book to lie on a drawing room table, and, as the profits arising from its sale are to go to the Museum fund, it is clearly the duty of every good townsman of Nottingham who owns a best parlour to provide himself with a copy." The reviewer for the *Nottingham Daily Guardian* 27 November 1876 ended his piece on the first edition rather cuttingly. "As a work of art, the book is only moderately successful. The photographs and plans, though extremely useful and interesting, are not very well executed, and the binding is, to our taste, as ugly as it is pretentious." However Hine had ensured that the Rt. Hon. W.E. Gladstone and F. Ouvry F.S.A., President of the Society of Antiquaries, received early copies, and their complimentary comments were used in advertising the book.

His activities as a conservationist and author brought Hine recognition from the Society of Antiquaries who elected him a fellow of the Society (F.S.A.) in 1876.

12. Into Retirement

Fairly comprehensive records exist for buildings in Nottingham after September 1874, and although Hine was into his sixties and engaged, initially on the Castle and the Shire Hall, an interesting and extensive range of assignments continued to come from his office. His son George appears to have given the practice some zest with his feeling for the Queen Anne Revival.

Several old clients needed to enlarge their premises: Thomas Adams's Stoney Street warehouse (1875), the Coppice Hospital (1880), R. Dickinson's sales shop (1885 Long Row and 1872 & 1887 Market Street), and W. and F. Dobson's Meadow Mills (1878-90). In Sherwood Rise he laid out seven roads for Thomas Leman between 1881-3: Hamilton Street (Road), Clinton Avenue, Herbert Road, Mayo Road, Claremont Road, Erskine Road and Elton Road. Several villas were built for Leman on these new roads.

In the flurry of building Board Schools after the Forster Education Act of 1870, Hine designed the Blue Bell Hill (1882), Carrington, (now Claremont Primary, 1883) and Stanley Road (1888) Board Schools. His son George was responsible for the Ilkeston Road Board School (1885) on the corner of Radford Boulevard. Hine's last major assignment was the Board School in Lovers' Lane, Newark, (1889), well designed with the now familiar Queen Anne detailing.

A few quality houses were erected. No. 2 Lucknow Drive (1886) had the shaped gables and decorative strapwork of Hine's Jacobean revival, while 428 Woodborough Road was a sturdy house for H. Heymann (1886). Several houses were built on Forest Road West (1880-84).

Of further streets: Gordon Street, Stewart Street and Burnaby Street were laid out in Basford (1885). Perhaps most surprising of all a series of terraces totalling 50 dwelling houses were put up in Crocus Street (1885) followed a few months later by 23 further dwelling houses and workshops on an adjoining site.

In the Park Estate Hine and Son continued to develop some of the remaining plots. These later designs of Hine's differ greatly from his earlier work and reflect the increasing influence in the provinces of Norman Shaw, J.J. Stevenson and the Queen Anne Revival. The houses are very decorative with heavy red pediments, swags and panels of terracotta. Several may be seen in Lenton Avenue, especially the splendid No. 17; a few earlier houses have 'Queen Anne' additions. However, the most imposing is No. 19 Park Terrace, perched precipitously on the edge of the Park Tunnel. Here, perhaps to celebrate the architect's continuing ingenuity, the house has the date 1881 and the initials T.C.H. in a bold terracotta panel. By 1887 Hine had seen the virtual completion of his original scheme. Earlier between 14-17 March 1877, just prior to the passing of the 1877 Borough Extension Act, Hine was in London with the Town Clerk, Samuel Johnson, and Alderman William George Ward (later that year first mayor of the enlarged Borough) to discuss the question of the Park's annexation.

Hine rarely took part in architectural competitions, but was tempted to enter one for the redevelopment of the area known as the 'Rookeries'. The Council declared this area on Long Row, between Greyhound Street and almost to Market Street, and reaching up to Parliament Street, an unhealthy area in the spring of 1881. In May 1881 the Council sent plans and full details to interested local architects, offering prizes of 50 and 25 guineas for those redevelopment schemes judged first and second in order of merit.

Entries were sent in under fanciful noms de plume; the architects' real names were submitted in separate envelopes. Hine's entry, one of nine sets of plans received, was sent as "Just What's Wanted". No drawings survive of these entries but descriptions appeared in the *Nottingham Daily Express on* 4 October 1881. Under a headline "The Proposed Improvements in Nottingham" Hine's entry was the first considered. It had as its central feature a single storey public covered market. This would be approached through an archway on Long Row and then via a wide street branching right and left in shape like a tuning fork. In front of the market there would be a crescent of spacious shops. Along the sides of the market and facing Parliament Street would be four blocks of shops, with a narrower street providing service access to the rear of these shops. The Long Row archway would be flanked on either side by large well-appointed hotels, which would preserve the traditional piazza of the Row. The writer's surprisingly modern verdict pointed out the land was "too valuable for use as a market, especially as we already possessed one of the finest in the kingdom" and "the entrances to the new streets from the Row [are] such as would cause frequent blocks in traffic." Hine's entry was unsuccessful; perhaps he had some consolation as the first prize went to the architectural practice of two of his former pupils, Robert Evans and William Jolley under the name "Sweetness and Light"- but it was never implemented.

Gradually, during the 1880s as he approached and passed his three score years and ten, Hine eased off his workload. He ceased to put in the long hours, 9am-6pm then l0pm-2am, of his 'younger' days.

In much of his work, son George increasingly became the agent. For example, George had supervised the extension of the Coppice Hospital (1880) and in 1883-84, representing his father on behalf of the Newcastle Estate, negotiated the diverting of the River Leen into the canal for the purpose of forming Lenton (later Castle) Boulevard.

This is one of several Christmas cards Hine designed to send to friends. This card was drawn in his 84th year; no doubt the subject chosen is a celebration of 50 years in the family home at 25 Regent Street. The cards were professionally printed, in this year 1896, he sent out 180 Christmas cards! (L.S.L.)

Although the Chapel of Saint Paul at Clumber House was commissioned from Hine by the 5th Duke of Newcastle, his untimely death in 1864 meant it was erected for his heir the 6th Duke. It was 'completed' in 1867, and demolished by the 7th Duke prior it being replaced by another grander chapel by Bodley & Garner (1886-9). Thus with a life span of less than 20 years it must rank as Hine's shortest lived building! (L.S.L.)

George had designed several buildings under his own name, whilst in the family partnership. Encouraged by his father in 1875, he entered and won the first prize of £100 for his proposals for a new Lunatic Asylum in Nottingham at Mapperley costing close to £30,000. Thereafter, and whilst still with his father, he entered open competitions for a number of asylums. He won further first prizes at Woodford, Essex, (1887), Charminster, Dorset, (1890), Ryhope, Sunderland, (1891), and a second prize for Taunton, (1891). Unsuccessful entries were made for Derby, (1884) and Maidstone, (1887).

In 1890, at the age of 77, Thomas Chambers Hine retired. George moved to London and continued through his newly established practice to enhance his reputation in his chosen field. He was extraordinarily successful in competitions; in seven years he took part in twelve competitions for asylums and other important buildings. He was awarded first place in seven and second in the remaining five. It was this rather specialised architectural prowess which resulted in G.T. Hine being appointed as Consulting Architect to H. M. Commissioners in Lunacy in 1897, a post he held for 20 years, during which time he voluntarily relinquished competition work. In 1898 he was elected an Honorary Member of the Medico-Psychological Association of Great Britain and Ireland, a rare honour for a non-medical man. George died "in harness" on 25 April 1916.

In his later years T.C. Hine enjoyed researching and preparing illustrated broadsheets, some of which he had printed for friends. Their titles included 'Jottings of a Jaunt in Germany' (1882), 'The Past, Present and Possible Future of the Church of Saint Mary, Nottingham' (1881), '28 Bits of Bygone Nottingham' (1890) and the ingenious Hine Family Genealogical Wheel (c.1893). Retirement gave him more time to spend with pen, pencil and brush.

He recorded the interior of churches and relics unearthed in excavation; he often illuminated letters to friends with thumbnail sketches of artefacts and ruins. For a number of years he designed his own Christmas cards: he noted, "On 22 December 1896 sent 180 Christmas cards." Sometimes he gave of his considerable experience, one notable occasion being the preparation of plans for the possible conversion of the old Baptist Meeting House in Plumptre Place into a parochial hall for St. Mary's Church (1893). He appeared very willing to discuss topics of interest, historical and architectural, with other amateur historians; indeed with anyone interested in the past of Nottingham. His welcome was uniformly warm and spontaneous and he was very willing to let friends browse in his extensive library. He took no direct interest in political or municipal affairs, although in his earlier days he had entertained politicians, nobility, noted architects, and land agents among others at 25 Regent Street.

On Monday, February 6th, 1899, after a brief, but painful illness, Thomas Chambers Hine died at his home on Regent Street, the house he had built for his family over half a century earlier. He was in his 86th year. His wife Mary had died at the close of 1893. They had three sons: George Thomas, James Augustus, Harry, and four daughters Mary Melicent, Sarah Alice, Emily, and Annie. Among the family and civic mourners at his funeral a few days later was Mr Watson Fothergill, architect.

Hine's grave in the Rock Cemetery on Mansfield Road was long anonymous, marked only by something akin to a rusty metal finial about a metre high. In the mid 1980s work by Family First exposed a stone base with inscriptions relating to T. C., his wife Mary and his youngest daughter Annie (d. 1919). The ornamented cross was cleaned of rust and painted black. A three part stained glass window in the south west corner of the nave at St. Mary's Church, in the Lace Market carries the inscription "To the Glory of God and in loving memory of Thomas Chambers Hine FSA born 1813 died 1899 and Mary his wife born 1813 died 1893. This window is dedicated by their children."

The contents of 25 Regent Street were auctioned by Neale and Son on July 4th and 5th, 1899. Hine's effects were valued at £28,459-17-8d. Probate was granted on March 10th, 1899, to George Thomas Hine, architect, James Augustus Hine, factory inspector, Harry Hine, surgeon, and Annie Hine, spinster. Hine's estate, which included houses such as 1. and 3. Newcastle Drive was wound up by his grandson C. Carew-Webb.

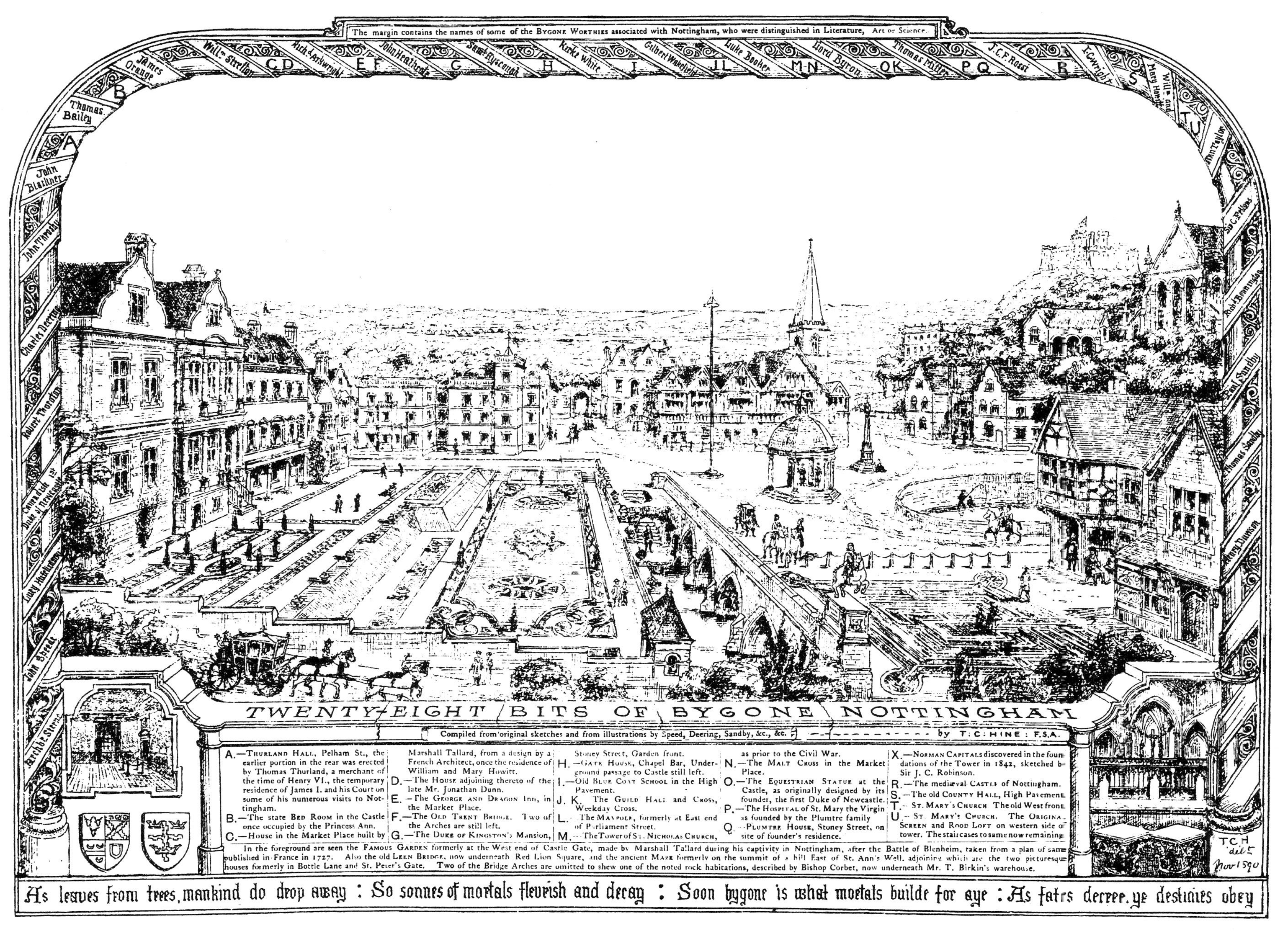

Hine, the antiquarian's interpretation of "Twenty-Eight Bits of Bygone Nottingham" dated "Nov 1890". Another version in colour exists. (L.S.L.)

Acknowledgements

I wish to thank the staffs of the Local Studies Library, Angel Row, Nottingham and the Nottinghamshire County Record Office. The late Professor M.W. Barley and the late Mr. Keith Train checked the manuscript of the first edition and gave freely of their unrivalled knowledge of local buildings. Stephen Best has, as always, been willing to listen and discuss ideas. Trevor Buck's work on Alexandra Park has been very useful. Pauline Heathcote, F.N. Hoskins and Geoffrey Oldfield have provided information. Patsy and Stephen kindly read the manuscript and made helpful suggestions. The Bedfordshire County Record Office supplied details about Cranfield Court. Church Lukas Architecture & Design kindly provided a drawing of Steegman's warehouse, Plumptre Street.

The cover photograph of the "Adams" Building, Stoney Street is reproduced by courtesy of Martine Hamilton Knight. I have retained photographs by David Lovesy and G. L. Roberts, the rest are by the author. The drawings are reproduced with the permission of either the Local Studies Librarian (L.S.L.) or the Principal Archivist, Nottinghamshire Archive Office (N.R.O.).

19 Park Terrace 1881, one of Hine's final flourishes in the Park Estate.

Printed by Parker & Collinson Ltd. (incorporating DESA Design). 0115 942 0140